THE *A*LPHABET OF
*D*ESIRE

New York University Press
gratefully acknowledges the support of
Madeline and Kevin Brine
in making these awards possible.

New York University Press Prizes for Fiction and Poetry

The New York University Press Prizes for Fiction and Poetry acknowledge fine works of literature and poetry by writers whose work, though often already a known quantity, remains unrecognized relative to the quality and ambition of their writing.

Past winners of the awards are:

Indentation and Other Stories
Joe Schall
(fiction)

Living with Strangers
Robert Schirmer
(fiction)

Let the Dog Drive
David Bowman
(fiction)

*The Lost and Found and
    Other Stories*
Anne Marsella
(fiction)

Cannibal
Terese Svoboda
(fiction)

Bird Self Accumulated
Don Judson
(fiction)

Bye-Bye
Jane Ransom
(fiction)

The Ruins
Trace Farrell
(fiction)

Crazy Water: Six Fictions
Lori Baker
(short stories)

Sing, Sing, Sing
Bruce Murphy
(poetry)

Wild Brides
Laura Kasischke
(poetry)

Like Memory, Caverns
Elizabeth Dodd
(poetry)

*Man Living on a Side Creek and
    Other Poems*
Stephan Torre
(poetry)

Human Nature
Alice Anderson
(poetry)

Rodent Angel
Debra Weinstein
(poetry)

Flying Out with the Wounded
Anne Caston
(poetry)

Long Like a River
Nancy Schoenberger
(poetry)

In 1998 the jurors selected *The Marvelous Adventures of Pierre Baptiste, Father and Mother, First and Last* by Patricia Eakins and Barbara Hamby's collection of poems, *The Alphabet of Desire*.

THE ALPHABET OF DESIRE

Barbara Hamby

NEW YORK UNIVERSITY PRESS
New York and London

NEW YORK UNIVERSITY PRESS
New York and London

© 1999 by Barbara Hamby

Library of Congress Cataloging-in-Publication Data
Hamby, Barbara.
The alphabet of desire / Barbara Hamby.
p.   cm.
ISBN 0-8147-3597-5 (alk. paper)
ISBN 0-8147-3598-3 (pbk. : alk. paper)
I. Title.
PS3558.A4216 A79 1999
811'.54—ddc21   98-58063
CIP

New York University Press books are printed on acid-free paper,
and their binding materials are chosen for strength and durability.

Manufactured in the United States of America

10 9 8 7 6 5 4 3 2 1

For my mother and father

CONTENTS

ACKNOWLEDGMENTS

Boulevard: "Footbinding as a Way of Life," "Irony Waltz," and "Zugzwang Amore"

Columbia: "Ode to Warts"

Five Points: "Hey, Udine!," "Uccello, Filippo Lippi, Leonardo," "Ode on My Bitterness," "Ode to the Lost Luggage Warehouse at the Rome Airport," "Ode to Black and White Movies," "Beriberi," and "Kamehameha Drive-in, 25 Years Later"

Green Mountains Review: "Elliot and I Discuss Eliot via *Macbeth*" and "Midnight on the Piazza della Signoria"

The Iowa Review: "Millennium Rave"

The Journal: "Cruelty" and "Dad, Dave, Deluge, Death"

The Kenyon Review: "Ode to Public Bathrooms" and "Thinking of Galileo"

Laurel Review: "Ode to Breath"

The Ohio Review: "Ode to Castrati" and "Reichsführer Blues"

The Paris Review: "Ode to Money," "Ode to Teeth," and "Ode to Untoward Dreams"

Parnassus: "With Sonya" and "Achtung, My Princess, Goodnight"

Quarterly West: "Mr. Pillow"

The Southern Review: "The Chicken-Wire Girls," "Ode to Italian Fruit," "The Dream of the Red Drink," "Ode to Insects," "X-ray of Your Brain at 4 A.M.," and "So Long, Roy"

Southern Poetry Review: "Blood" and "The Word"

Verse: "Yellow Fever"

Western Humanities Review: "Ode on My Wasted Youth"

I would like to thank the National Endowment for the Arts for support during the period I wrote the poems in this book and the Macdowell Colony for acres of uninterrupted time.

I can never express my gratitude to Richard Howard for his generosity and encouragement, nor my love and appreciation to Phyllis Moore for her close readings and intelligent suggestions. I would also like to thank Mark Pietralunga and Karen Myers for two glorious summers in Italy that were the inspiration of many of these poems and Megan Holmes for her insights into Italian Renaissance and Baroque art. Thanks also to Allen Woodman for giving me the idea for the title of this book and for being his illustrious self. And to my husband, David Kirby, my slavish devotion for being the comma czar and for making every day poetic.

I.

I can do you blood and love without the rhetoric,
and I can do you blood and rhetoric without the love,
and I can do you all three concurrent or consecutive
but I can't do you love and rhetoric without the blood.
Blood is compulsory.

—TOM STOPPARD, *Rosenkrantz and Guildenstern Are Dead*

The Word

In the beginning was the word, fanning out into syllables
    like a deck of cards on a table in Vegas,
litigious leafy parts fluttering into atoms and cells,
    genus and phylum, nouns, verbs,
elephants, orangutans, O Noah, you and your philological
    filing and filling of arks, gullets, daughters.
In the beginning was the word and it was as big
    as Aretha Franklin after "Chain of Fools,"
long as your mother's memory of all your misdeeds,
    wide as Jerusalem, a fat-lady-in-the-circus word,
a Siberia, a steppe, a savanna, a stretch, a Saturnalia,
    the party at the end of the world.
In the beginning was the word and we knew which way it went:
    left to right in English, right to left
in Hebrew, an orientation so profound that sexual climax
    is coming in all right-moving languages
going in those advancing left, though in the moment
    we rarely know whether we're coming or going.
In the beginning was the word, small and perfect,
    a Hans Holbein miniature, a dormouse,
a gnat, a bee, a blink, a breath in the lungs
    of Jehovah, Brahman, the Buddha, Ra,
because all the big kahunas of the universe surfed
    in on the crest of that first wave,
and Thomas Edison said let there be light
    and the dinosaurs groaned in their graves,
and there was Albuquerque, late-night roadhouses,
    blues, cigarettes, fishnet stockings,
high-density sodium street lights that blot out the stars,
    cars, diners, the neon urban carnival before Lent,
and Marie Curie said let there be more light,
    and there was radium, radiant thermonuclear

incandescent explosions, Herr Einstein's dream,
  Herr Oppenheimer's furnace,
London burning with Hitler's fire, Dresden cremated
  in the answering flame, *Hiroshima mon amour.*
I ask you, what is this world with its polyglot delirium,
  its plainspoken, tight-assed, stumblebum euphoria?
Explain time, for I am fretting on the outskirts of Odessa,
  with Chekhov, with Eisenstein, with ten thousand martyrs
of unremembered causes, and we are cold, hungry,
  tired of playing Hearts.
Where are you, my minister of *informazione,* Comrade Surgeon,
  Mister Wizard, Gino Romantico?
Can you in your lingo ferret out the first word? Inspect
  your dialect for clues, my Marlowe, my Holmes,
your patois for signs, your pagan vernacular, your scatological
  cant, your murmuring river of carnal honey,
for in the beginning there was darkness until you came,
  my pluperfect anagram of erotic delight,
my wild-haired professor of vinissimo and mayhem,
  emperor of Urbino, incubator of rhythm, bright-eyed Apollo
of the late-night bacchanalia, and there was music,
  that heady martini of mathematics and beauty.
For I am empty, I am full, I am certain, I am not,
  for in the beginning there was nothing
and it was blank and indescribable,
  a wave breaking on the north shore of the soul,
but as every canyon aches for its sky, I burned for you
  with a fever, with a frenzy,
I was a woman craving a blaze, a flame,
  a five-alarm fire in my heart, in my bones,
my hair red as a hibiscus, like a burning bush,
  I was Moses screaming at God,
filaments of flame eating my eyes,
  my sex, the hard sweet apple of my mouth.

Millennium Rave

Let us go mad, my darlings, with news, information, facts,
the concupiscence of catastrophe, the evil thrill

of our present dilemma, the bright confederacy of all
that can go wrong, the bombs, my beauties, the grenades,

the undetonated chaos packed tight inside everyone
like Mae West in her cantilevered whalebone corset.

The buzz has it that our time is up, the rumble
is that no one cares, but the inside skinny betrays life

as robust with a kind of queasy charisma,
mean and attractive at the same moment,

like your no-good boyfriend who is Galahad
asleep, Quasimodo the rest of the time.

Let's storm the citadel of our own stupidity,
because this is gospel, my little Shih Tzus,

this is a telegram from Mount Olympus,
we are sailing on the Titanic, dressed to the nines,

doing the two-step, the tango, the soft shoe,
popping corks of Veuve Clicquot, and why not?

The iceberg cometh, the seas are rough,
hallelujah, a mighty fortress is our God.

Let us rhapsodize, my little pedal pushers,
over Gershwin, over Callas, over Blind Lemon Jefferson,

over boogie woogie, big band, Bartók, the blues.
Get out your bicycle, Herr Wittgenstein,

roll out your Lincoln, Mr. Kafka, you handsome
shivering hunk of paranoia and nerves.

Let's take a ride, Vincent, through the starry night,
in your rattletrap, in your rickshaw, in your acid yellow

1957 Chevy Deluxe with the convertible top.
Let's dish the dirt, my little birds of prey,

I have a bottle of gin but find adultery monotonous,
ditto incest. I want a story with magic, lemon zest,

a wedding cake of a story with butter and sugar
and eggs because I have a sweet tooth, a black hole,

a predilection for scandal and sandals, sling-backs
in silver and gold. Come to me, my little stool pigeons,

spill the beans to Auntie Em, Uncle Walt is in the barn
doing God knows what, but I have the whiff of something juicy

and you, my little blabbermouths, are just the ones
to clue me in, because you'd double-cross your grandmother

for a kick in the ass from someone who doesn't give a fig
for you. Uccello, old bird brain, where is your perspective now,

your mathematics, your converging lines? I'm in a twitter,
my sweets, in a flutter, a twist. You hippogriff, gorgon,

minotaur mounting a flailing virgin, don't pussyfoot around
with me, Pablo, I'm on to you, you fink, you spy,

squawk all you want, while I continue my rumba
with the infinite, my mambo with the spheres,

because I have a tip, a glimmer, an inkling, and while
the night remains dark and injurious, I will rave on.

Blood

While swilling gin at an elegant outdoor reception,
I look out on a sea of suits, and Maxine asks me,

"Who's Robert Johnson?" I know she's talking about one
of the other guests, but I've had a couple of drinks,

so I say, "Didn't he write "Love in Vain," but I'm thinking
"vein" the way I think "veil" when I hear "vale of tears,"

because in the middle of a crying jag tears can be a veil
between you and the world, as in those tiny mountain churches

in New Mexico or Ecuador with their painted wooden statues
of the Virgin who spouts tears of blood from her big blue

pinocchios and, looking out through her veil,
sees a swarm of peasants crowding around her image

in hopes she will intercede for them with God who seems
to have been in a really bad mood for a couple of thousand years,

and they're down on their knees, and you know they're saying,
We're Indians, for God's sake, we had nothing to do

with your son's death, don't blame us, we're so poor,
and the Vatican hasn't bought a good painting since

the Velázquez Pope by Francis Bacon, so give us a break,
we cry—I say "we" because I'm feeling the Indian blood

hot in my veins right now, and I want the Virgin
to do something about the pope, at least convince him

to let up on birth control. No, I want a war in heaven,
but that's my German blood coming out, and it can get riled up,

exercised, be prone to oratory, *Sieg heil* and so forth,
but that German blood is depressive, too, loves Wagner,

sobs in its schnitzel, regrets passion, because an exercised
heart is an organ perhaps too big for its cavity,

one prone to err, and though Robert Johnson is drinking
bourbon while conversing with a former liberal governor

of our great state, I'm sure he would join his darker,
more melancholy brother in saying something equally

unhopeful, because we have the blues tonight, every last
Teutonic-Indian on the planet. We are howling at the moon.

The Ex-Goddess Speaks

Here I am again, the anarchist sob sister
    of this opéra comique, aria shaky, high C
somewhere between St. Louis and Dubuque,

wahine extraordinaire, Pele spewing fire from the center
    of the earth, minx, cat, Boadicea,
a tigress who will tear your eyes out to feed her young.

I am the *dolce far niente* workaholic of your Capri
    dreams: blue water, blue eyes, blue heart
in my laughing mouth, the bête noire of every beauty,

time chasing her out of this mumbo jumbo paradise
    of mascara-frond palm trees. I'm high priestess
of the cult of insomnia, wide-eyed Amazon, vigilant,

hoarding canned corn and AK-47s. Call me Medusa,
    Cleopatra, a serious snake handler in search of a cobra,
a fang, a canine indentation into innocent flesh.

I'm the bourgeois dame with six double chins,
    one for each decade, fed by fresh cream
and Linzer torte, the Ausländer with a Baedeker,

looking for a Ghirlandaio, a Schongauer,
    a double transformation altarpiece in Colmar,
the anti-Frau wearied by the onslaught

of Kirche, Küche, Kinder, a cow with Vedantic udders,
    true-blue Brünnhilde in *Götterdämmerung,* the smart girl
in class, knowing the answer, biting her tongue.

I'm the morphine rich goddess of the Blue Spot tune,
    crooning a low aching arpeggio, scatting the skin
off men in business suits, bow ties,

Dorothy Parker after martini number four,
　　Amelia Earhart in a nosedive, Catherine the Great
in a syphilitic delirium. I'm the yenta

in every shtetl between Hoboken and hell,
　　I'm the harridan here to tell you to listen
to me because I know nothing, and nothing

is what you need. Empty your house, clean your attics,
　　send all your flotsam up in a tornado of chairs,
books, papers, TVs, to orbit Saturn as part of the stars

because there's no end of torture on our street:
　　flaying, defenestration, estrapade, the rack. Jumping
out the window of every day are the bromides,

the suicides, the ceremonial stabs in the back,
　　so where are my pills, my knives, my hanging rope?
I'm in a lynching mood, and my neck feels long and fine.

THE HUNTER

I'm persuaded the day will come when I'll lie motionless
as a falcon in a hunter's sack, fragments of iron

studding my reckless breast, the smell of the bag, dark
and gorgeous: dull garnets of blood, damp feathers, acrid

attar of carbon and smoke. Music could not save you,
nor the words that gather in my mouth like angry flames

of hope. I have swallowed your eyes, lived on them
for years, made them into coins for beggars, for bankers

in their mausoleums of flesh. With the wide sky
for flight, how have you tumbled into this bowl of ash?

With the long night for sleep, why have you squandered
your breath? We studied many maps for this desert expedition,

but they are useless now as confetti or rice, silent
as your mouth, once a dark plum, ripe with blood and sweet.

—in memory of Lynn Fiedeldey

The Chicken-Wire Girls

You can sing this to the tune of "Buffalo Gals,
    Won't You Come Out Tonight," a song
which I spent many insomniac hours in college
    trying to deconstruct in the solitude and squalor
of my graham-cracker-crumb-littered sheets.
    What is a buffalo gal?
A girl from Buffalo, New York? A girl
    who hunts buffalos and then later opens
a Wild West Show that travels around Europe?
    Or is she a big girl, a female
of majestic proportions, an Amazon,
    a statuesque creature, a goddess?
So that when in the passenger's seat of a car traveling west
    from Tallahassee, Florida, to New Orleans,
I see two cars moving as in a caravan, both driven
    by young women, and instead of glass
in the window on the driver's side
    there is chicken wire in both cars,
I can't help but call them the Chicken-Wire Girls
    and wonder what they are doing.
Let's start with fundamentals. They are driving west.
    It appears they are driving west
with all their earthly possessions
    in not-very-new Japanese import sedans
that are worse for wear and have chicken wire
    instead of glass in their windows.
What would Sherlock Holmes make of these two cars,
    a large mutt in the passenger's seat of one,
as I recall? Are they looking for adventure, running
    from bad boyfriends, or, more interestingly, the law?
They are girls after my own heart, bohemian vegetarians
    from their looks, though being real Americans

they probably have eaten their share of hot dogs
    and chicken pot pie.
I say they are going to New Orleans, the most
    interesting city until Santa Fe,
but who's to know? Not me, that's for sure, because we leave
    those rusty, beat-up Toyotas in the dust,
but still I have so many questions, such as:
    Why is it called chicken wire, anyway?
Why not poultry filament or rooster cable?
    And how is anything named in the first place?
I christen them duck-barricade girls or pullet-fence girls
    or *les filles du filament du poulet,*
which sounds like an opera by Donizetti with lyrics
    by Groucho Marx. No *nom de théâtre*
is quite right, and that night as I lie
    in the motel bed drifting off to sleep in the icy
air-conditioned room, thinking about my misspent youth,
    the melody comes to me, "Chicken-wire girls,
won't you come out tonight and dance by the light of the moon?"
    It's an *On the Road* kind of thing,
but as time passes I treasure those aimless days more,
    when I'd read Nietzsche for fun
and think about Time, Art, Death, and Nothingness,
    especially Nothingness. At twenty,
one's mind is a chicken coop of ideas, hope, fear,
    and you can see why drugs are so appealing
because your mind's such a mess anyway, who would know
    the difference? But time changes everything,
it either takes you out or makes you afraid,
    but not my girls, they pull their cars to the side
of I-10 and with their dogs dance in the drifts
    of black-eyed susans and wild mallow
that line the roadside, forgetting the past
    back in Pensacola, Panama City, Jacksonville,

and pirouette down the white lines of the highway
　　as if there were no road ahead, no apartments,
ramshackle houses, dead-end jobs, lovers, children
　　in Baton Rouge, Austin, Albuquerque, L.A.

With Sonya

I've only walked out on two movies in my life, the first
The Story of O. When the Marquis started inserting those rings

in O's labia, I was out the door. I mean, really, wouldn't
another metaphor have done as well? The second

was a musical by Peter Bogdanovich, starring Burt Reynolds
and Cybill Shepherd dancing and singing. Within the first five

minutes I bolted to the theater next door, showing *Chinatown.*
Now *there* was a movie, equal parts beauty and squalor,

amour and revenge, ardor and restlessness. For years my brother
would turn to me, say, "Forget it, Jake. It's Chinatown,"

and I knew what he meant. Okay, so Roman Polanski's a shit,
he shouldn't fuck thirteen-year-old girls, no matter how horrible

his childhood was in Nazi Poland, but think about *Repulsion,*
that last scene, the photograph in which young Catherine

Deneuve is sitting away from the rest of the family, a little
twisted even then, or *Macbeth* with sublime Francesca Annis

stalking naked through the castle, trying to rub out
that damned spot. Hitchcock was no Boy Scout, nor were Chaplin

or Ford, who made John Wayne look tragic and luminescent,
which rates right up there with the Wedding at Cana

in the water-into-wine department. Miracles aside, even pathetic
movies have their pleasures: sitting in that big dark room

while the film rolls over you like the river of life. I love
a marginal movie; one good line or actor is all it takes

to hook me. So recently, as I settled down to watch a film
of which I had few expectations, and two women I know

sat down beside me in the crowded theater, and while I talked
to them I spotted an old boyfriend, who always tries to act

like we're friends, so I scrunched down in my seat,
and then I saw my husband's first wife and her Neanderthal

husband, who makes our lives miserable whenever he can,
and I was chatting to the women about *Uncle Vanya,*

how in any production I begin to weep as soon as Sonya
appears on stage because I can never forget her last speech

to Vanya, you know, "We must go on living." They looked at me
as though I was either crazy or stupid, because they hated

the recent film by Louis Malle, but then the lights went down,
the movie started. It wasn't very good, though the leading man

was handsome and a delicate blonde played his wife with a mix
of moxie and tristesse and the villain was despicable,

so on a very minor level I could enjoy it—that is, no labia
piercing and no song and dance by those who can neither sing

nor dance. Then the woman next to me began making sounds
as sexually repulsive developments unfolded on the screen,

and since the story was set in 18th-century Scotland,
this was pretty much all the time, and she was hissing,

snickering mirthlessly, bringing me back from the Highlands
to the theater, which is not where I wanted to be,

or I would have stayed home and opened a new pack of cards
or telephoned my mother, who is tolerant and funny

and taught me how to act in public, which means when Burt
Reynolds puts on his tap shoes or the Marquis starts polishing

his vaginal piercing implements, leave the theater,
have a beer and let the morally corrupt enjoy their pathetic

divertimenti. On the screen the actors are hacking
each other with swords, the fabulous sneering villain

piercing the hero's arm, but I'm not in Scotland
and will never be, because the woman next to me

is making a sound like air being let out of a tire,
and I'm in that room with Sonya. I want to walk out

and I'm talking about my life, worse than any B movie—
ragged plot, supporting players who couldn't act

their way out of a paper bag—yet I can't
leave because though the dialogue could have been written

by Daffy Duck and the plot devices engineered
by Rasputin, it's my movie and I have to see how it ends.

Beriberi

For five or six years I haven't been really emotional,
I mean rip-roaring mad. Where did my anger go?

Did I lose it one afternoon walking home from work
or misplace it as my grandmother once did her teeth,

later finding them in the pantry behind cans of beans?
The nearest I come to emotion these days is panic,

as when the pilot of our plane tried to land
in the middle of Tropical Storm Beryl. For God's sake,

it had a name. Don't they have a rule in pilot school?
Rule number 437? You idiot, if a storm has a name,

don't try to land. When we touched down the first time,
the woman behind me said, "Thank you, Jesus,"

which quickly turned into, "Oh, my God,"
because we went right back up only to try it again,

the plane shaking like a little girl with fire ants
in her shoes. I have never been so aware of my own heart,

how small it is, how hard it works. All the way back to Tampa,
I listened to my body toil like a farmer in the fields,

each breath plowing through my lungs and into the blood
like an iron blade, each thought painful, not dead

but not really alive either. In my younger days
I was quite the little Sturm-und-Dranger. I remember

when we were first married, that fight we had.
There were so many rules, and I didn't seem to know

any of them, so one day I snapped and stalked
through the house apologizing: I'm sorry, I beg

your pardon, Excuse me, Forgive me, It's my fault,
Oh, I *am* a dunce, How can you bear it, living

with such a moron? My boyfriend had turned into
Family Man, which involved meal planning, child care,

and IRAs and I'm not talking about the Irish group
that blows up train stations. More than anything

I wanted my boyfriend back. What evil spirit
made you become that voodoo Ward Cleaver who suddenly

wanted to act married? Then something changed, both of us,
I suppose, because you are your beautiful self again.

Did we break a mirror or eat potato salad
that had been too long in the sun? Be careful, darling.

I know I say it too much. When you leave the house
without me, who will watch for the odd malevolent truck,

falling trees, the lightning? From Paris, Madame de Sévigné
wrote to her daughter in Provence: "My dear,

I must be persuaded of your real affection for me
since I am still alive." Wretched hours that separate us,

as if an essential nutrient were missing, as in the deficiency
of vitamin B1, a disease characterized by great weakness

and called beriberi, which translated is, "I cannot."
I cannot imagine a greater pleasure than to lie in bed

at night and listen to you breathe, the dark room around me
like a veil. Sometimes I wake and wonder if I am dead,

but I must be alive since you are breathing and your heart
is beating, filled with blood, empty, then full again.

Mr. Pillow

I'm watching a space invasion movie in which a wife
tells her pilot husband that she hugs his pillow

when he is away. Well, sure, every girl does that,
takes comfort in Mr. Pillow when her boyfriend is gone,

but not when Bela Lugosi is breaking the lock
on your prefab fifties bungalow. You fight him off,

but he still knows where you are, and the police don't care,
or they're bumbling incompetents, and your husband is big

but not too bright; let's face it, he's not even a pilot,
he's an actor and not a very good one at that,

and what Mr. Pillow lacks in facial definition,
he more than makes up for in his cuddle quotient,

although there is the genital dilemma. Poor Mr. Pillow
is sadly lacking in that area. I hate staying in hotels

because of the king-size beds. I did not get married
not to sleep with my husband. If I had, Mr. Pillow

would do just as well, because he's certainly never sarcastic
and he'd let me run my credit cards up as high as I want

and never make me save for retirement, so I have to admit
that I have, on occasion, used Mr. Pillow to make my husband

jealous, as when he's sitting on his side of an enormous
hotel bed, way over in a far island of dull yellow

lamplight, reading a fascinating article on flyfishing
in Antarctica or the destruction of life as we know it

on Planet Earth, and I turn to Mr. Pillow, hold him tight
and say, "Oh, Mr. Pillow, you know what a woman needs

from a man." Getting no response from the outer reaches
of Patagonia, I whisper, "Oh, Mr. Pillow, you make me blush."

"Would you shut up about Mr. Pillow?" "Oh, Mr. Pillow!"
I say as he flies across the room, and I get just what I want

and maybe what I deserve. Sometimes it's so difficult
to make these distinctions. Puritanism dies hard,

and if there are ghouls lurking in the yard, who's to say
they have any less right to be here than we do in our cozy

little beds all the while looking at the closet door, thinking,
Where are the cannibals, where do those zombies live?

Paper

Smooth as an egg slipping through a hen's cloaca,
nourishing as bread or milk, integral as bone,

skeleton of everything we write, folded by Japanese
into pleated swans, snipped by school children

into snowflakes, precious as pearls, unstrung,
unworn, cold as Christmas morning in Norway, radiant

as an albino walking down Fourteenth Street
on a July afternoon, transparent as a phantom,

alabaster sheet of nothingness, Sartre's old friend,
tragic as ivory minus its dear pachyderm, addictive

as cocaine, fallible as chalk on a board of equations,
as if numbers could explain the world, as if words

could light the room where a mother sits with her dying
child, pale as her face, waiting for the black ink of dawn.

Cut

The first cut is the surprise because it doesn't hurt
till later when you're over the initial spurt of blood

and the shock of seeing the inside of your body,
so wet and uninviting, like a closed society

that wants nothing to do with you, cuts you, in fact.
Can you be on the outs with yourself or are you simply

on the outs with your body? But what are we if not our bodies,
at least to some extent, because we drape ourselves on our forms

the way celebrants hook berries and paper angels
on fir trees at Xmas. I love that X, like a cut itself

into the mystery of the dominant cabal. X marks the spot.
In French it sounds like the cry of a mouse, eeks,

and the last three letters—eeks, i grec, zed—
ring out as if a mild curse, like Jesus, Mary and Joseph,

the latter two the putative parents of X, who said,
"I am the Way, the Truth, and the Light,"

which I have always read to mean not his physical corpus
was those terrific things but his state of consciousness.

That "I" is the problem, but what else could he say,
"This state of consciousness is the Way, the Truth, etc."

Not very poetic, what? For several years my television repairman
referred to himself in conversation as "this person,"

as in "This person thinks your picture tube should be replaced,"
and I thought he was a little nutty, but he was good

at what he did, so who cared? It's like the form of English
called E-prime that seeks to expunge the being verbs

from speech, and this person can see it would prove
difficult to accomplish as being is so fundamental to our daily,

if not conscious, then unconscious endeavors, and Hamlet
would be fresh out of luck. What would he say, To exist

or not to exist? Eeks, I grec, Zed—no euphony there!
To delete being from language would leave us with a panoply

of pure activity and no spin, like chickens pecking at the dirt,
cornless, that is, without the very kernel of life.

You could say, I love you, but who would love whom,
if there were no being? What would you love

if you were the "who," not to mention the "whom"? Dull rustless
days filled with dishwashing and car buying and other worthy

if tedious endeavors until lit with the poesie of philosophy,
ontologically speaking, to wit, twit, tweet, toot, Toulouse-

Lautrec painting the girls at the Moulin Rouge, their mouths
like cuts in the canvas, red and entrance into the treacherous

tunnel of the body, a cadaver lit with the light of the I
or the not-I, depending on one's position, but hoping to be

with the TV repairmen and messiahs in the true Eden
of the not-I, said the pussy cat to the little red hen.

Hey, Udine!

The first time five scruffy boys shouted it at our car
we were happy, knowing Italian schools were not slacking

in the instruction of the divine discipline of geography
and that the rental firm in Rome had not given us a car

to drive to the nefarious south that marked us as patsies
or, worse, gullible *americani* but that the UD on our license

meant we came from a small city in the north between Trieste
and Venice. However, our happiness was short-lived

because we were lost, the highway on the map having expired
in the middle of nowhere, and we wanted to be somewhere

or at least somewhere with a restaurant, and when the boys
shouted, "Hey, OO-dee-nay," we wondered if the rocky track

could possibly lead anywhere. Actually, it did not,
but we blundered on to Bari where we saw a stadium

like a silver spaceship hovering on the coastal plain.
The next day at the caverns of Castellana, at a carpark

a man shouted, "Hey, OO-dee-nay," and we began to think
we were from Udine. We imagined it a combination

of Vicenza and Venice, watery but with long slopes
of green meadows. We'd live just outside the city

in a Palladian villa, run down but with a sweep of stairs
like Aphrodite's eyebrow. For certainly we are not from Puglia,

the boot heel of Italy, where people stare as if we
just stepped off that spaceship. We talk about having cards made

that say, "Here's a photo, it'll last longer," like holy cards,
but with photos of our grinning extraterrestrial faces

instead of the saints. We are gloriously out of place.
I go into a bathroom, and I am the tallest woman

by six inches. I think of saying, "I have a sister
who is six one. If you think I'm tall, you ought to see Maria,"

or on the street with my husband, "If you think he's blond,
you'll faint when you see Maria." One night my mother and I

were walking with Maria to the Waikiki Shell
to lie on the grass under the stars and listen to Dvorák's

Symphony no. 9, and as we walked every man we passed
turned to stare, as a boy in Lecce pivots to gawk

through thick glasses as we walk into town to take our seat
on the Piazza Sant'Oronzo to watch the *passegiata:*

hulking boys in black leather, girls in short architectural
skirts, grandmothers in black strolling arm in arm

with stooped husbands. People pass, we drink our *aperitivi,*
and the moon rises like a spotlight on the amphitheater

excavated in the twenties, littered now with used syringes,
tufts of wildflowers, the effluvia of Fiats, *la vita moderna,*

which we share with such terror and relish and to which
we'll soon return in Udine or wherever it is we live.

THINKING OF GALILEO

When, during a weekend in Venice while standing
    with the dark sky above the Grand Canal
exploding in arcs of color and light,

a man behind me begins to explain
    the chemical composition of the fireworks
and how potassium-something-ate and sulfur catalyze

to make the gold waterfall of stars cascading
    in the moon-drunk sky, I begin to understand why
the Inquisition tortured Galileo

and see how it might be a good thing for people
    to think the sun revolves around the earth.
You don't have to know how anything works

to be bowled over by beauty,
    but with an attitude like mine we'd still be swimming
in a sea of smallpox and consumption,

not to mention plague, for these fireworks
    are in celebration of the Festival of the Redentore,
or Christ the Redeemer, whose church on the other side

of the canal was built after the great plague
    of 1575 to thank him for saving Venice,
though by that time 46,000 were dead,

and I suppose God had made his point if indeed he had one.
    The next morning, Sunday, we take the vaporetto
across the lagoon and walk along

the Fondamenta della Croce, littered
    with the tattered debris of spent rockets
and Roman candles, to visit the Church of the Redentore

by Palladio. The door is open for mass,
　　and as I stand in the back, a miracle occurs:
after a year of what seems to be nearly futile study,

I am able to understand the Italian of the priest.
　　He is saying how important it is
to live a virtuous life, to help one's neighbors,

be good to our families, and when we err
　　to confess our sins and take communion.
He is speaking words I know: *vita, parlare, resurrezione.*

Later my professor tells me the holy fathers
　　speak slowly and use uncomplicated constructions
so that even the simple can understand Christ's teachings.

The simple: well, that's me, as in one for whom
　　even the most elementary transaction is difficult,
who must search for nouns the way a fisherman

throws his net into the wide sea, who must settle
　　for the most humdrum verbs: I am, I have, I go, I speak,
and I see nothing is simple, even my desire to strangle

the man behind me or tell him that some things
　　shouldn't be explained, even though they can be,
because most of the time it's as if we are wandering

lost in a desert, famished, delirious,
　　set upon by wild lions, our minds blank with fear,
starving for a crumb, any morsel of light.

THE DREAM OF THE RED DRINK

This story begins, as they so often do, with heartbreak.
I am at a party for a young man whose wife has left him,
    so he's abandoning graduate school to join the navy.
There is a lot of despair at this gathering,
    the young man's and the impoverished students'
and, of course, mine, which has less to do with money
    and more to do with time,
which is running out, in case you haven't noticed.
And then there is the red drink.

Our host looks as if he has just stepped out
    of a Trollope novel, a nineteenth-century cleric
in rumpled chinos and a tee shirt.
    He and a friend have driven to Georgia
to buy grain alcohol and have mixed it with red Kool-Aid
    in a styrofoam container on the back porch.
Later when this party is famous, I learn the red drink
    eventually ate through the styrofoam,
but this was not discovered until the next day
    or maybe the next week when heads had finally cleared.
My host warns me not to drink much.
I don't, but I drink enough.

I don't know anyone at this party but the red drink
    makes me intrepid.
I talk to many people, make jokes, see God.
How many times can you see God before you realize
    his face is different every time?
Is this a revelation? Maybe.
Not only do I see God, but I see through him
    to the other side, though probably it's a vision
    of cerebral matter being sloughed off,
and I have a tête-à-tête with my most persistent epiphany,

that is, life is nothing, *rien, nada, niente.*
I find it incredibly comforting to know
    the world is transparent,
    insubstantial, without meaning.
I think of Niels Bohr's assertion that there is no deep
    reality, and I know exactly what he means.
I am looking through the woman I am talking to,
    seeing through her
    to the soft bank of azalea bushes behind.
It's a nice effect, rather like a double exposure.

My husband is at this party, but I am avoiding him
    for a reason I can't really remember.
Oh, I remember, but it's too tedious to go into here.
I look at this man whom I love to distraction
    and wonder how he can be so utterly dense,
and I know if I say anything he will say
    I've had too much to drink, which is entirely correct,
and that there's alcoholism in my family, but show me a family
    that doesn't have a drinker or two. . . .
My beloved is in a cluster of beautiful students
    who think he's marvelous, which he is.
Wait a minute, girls, I could tell you things,
    but the red drink has turned ethereal on me,
and it's two-thirty in the morning and the young man
    who's going into the navy is delirious or dead,
and the lovely students have disappeared
    into their enchanted student hovels.

So we leave and the car seems flimsy, as if made from
    cardboard, like the East German cars about which
I saw a documentary in a hotel room in Tampa:
    after World War II the East Germans didn't have any steel,
so they made cars out of cotton wool compressed
    between layers of organic plastic

that has proved to be almost completely unbiodegradable.
I look out into the night and think, this could be East Berlin,
    except it so obviously isn't, unless magnolias
and enormous oaks dripping with Spanish moss have been sighted
    on the Alexanderplatz.
But we are in motion and I sit in my seat, pulled through
    the night as if by a magnet
to an intersection in which I see that a low-slung black
    Oldsmobile will run a red light
and plow into my side of our flimsy East German car
    and the metaphysical and the physical worlds will have
to come to some kind of decision about my corporeal frame,
    and I think that maybe I don't want to walk
    into that good night just yet.

I say to my husband, "That black car's not going to stop,"
and he slows down, even though we have the green light,
    because I have authority in my voice,
authority bestowed on me by the red drink; in fact, I believe
    the red drink has made me slightly psychic,
    because the black car doesn't stop.
We watch it sail through the deserted early-morning
    intersection with wonder and astonishment,
    or at least I do
for Death has passed me by, its chariot zooming toward Perry,
    Florida, driven by a laughing young man with an Elvis
    haircut and his blonde teenaged girlfriend.

Time passes, probably a few minutes, but it seems
    interminable hours have stretched out before us.
We continue through the now-empty intersection,
    down an oak-lined street,
and turn to drive through the park,
    but a red fox is in the middle of the rumpled
asphalt and stares into our headlights.

He has a message for me and for my husband
and the pretty spellbound students
    and our Trollopian host
and the unconscious soon-to-be ensign,
    and I should be able to hear it clearly,
but I'm too giddy with being alive,
    my arms still chilled from the sleeve of death.

II. The Alphabet of Desire

Let us give each other complete happiness, and let us be sure that as many times as we satisfy our desires, they will be born anew.

—GIACOMO CASANOVA, *The History of My Life*, Volume 2, Chapter 6

All life is suffering. All suffering is caused by desire.

—THE BUDDHA, The first and second noble truths

ACHTUNG, MY PRINCESS, GOOD NIGHT

Arrivederci, Cinderella, your goose is cooked, grilled,
burned to be precise, blistered, while you, nestled in your

crumbling necropolis of love, think, who am I?
Delores del Rio? No, nothing so déclassé, yet

even your mice have deserted you, little pipsqueaks,
fled to serve your stepsisters, dedicated now to

good works, a soup kitchen, if you can imagine. What is this
heresy of ugliness that has overtaken the world?

I am Beauty, you scream. Wrong fairy tale, and
just so you don't forget, size sixes are not enough in this

karaoke culture, and even here you have to do more than
lip sync "Begin the Beguine," "My Funny Valentine,"

"Mona Lisa," "Satisfaction," because you can't get no,
no, no, no, consummation, so to speak. Sex is kaput,

over, married a decade, three litters of neurasthenic
princes, your figure shot, not to mention your vagina. Don't

quote me on that you cry, my public can't bear very much
reality. Who can? Yet there it is staring you in the face.

Scram, vamoose, la cucaracha, cha cha cha. Admit it, you're
tired of this creepy pedestal, the pressed pleats,

undercooked chicken, Prince Embonpoint and his cheesy
Virna Lisi look-alike mistress with her torpedo chest. Auf

Wiedersehen to this stinking fairy-tale life, this pack-rat
Xanadu built on the decomposing carcasses of girlish hope.

Yes, all your best friends, all your gorgeous diamonds are cubic
zirconias, but flashing like the real thing, as if you'd know.

BEELZEBUB ON THE PROWL

Anti-Christ, anti-matter—presenting the 20th century
    under the big top, the flip top, the bebop
babble of astronomy, astrology, palmistry, the hand tattoo,
    quantum voodoo echoing in the high trapeze.
Check your palms for your deepest self, consider the stars
    for tomorrow's news, split the atomic
deck for your next step into the freak show, the peep show,
    the postindustrial creep show,
elephants of revelation parading in the dust while Lucifer—
    Lord Gamma Ray, the Marquis de Tormentazione—
flicks his whip at the big cats, their eyes a dark continent
    of hate where we drown in the rolling
Ganges of tribal cant, rodomontade of revival-tent lizards,
    hex of half-baked
homeopathic salvation. So we're sick, we're still at the circus,
    having a ball, drawing blood, making money,
inserting something into every available orifice, and doesn't
    Satan look sexy in his jodhpurs, his
juju moving multitudes, his mojo working miracles,
    or so it seems from our place in the
kingdom of the one-watt bulb, in the high karmic bleachers,
    where it's dim but bright enough to see
loaves turning into something, who knows what at this distance—
    sardines, mackerel—old Beelzebub,
milking the scene, bilking the bozos, tricking the horde
    with his sleight of hand
napalm. We leave the coliseum thinking, *Where's our skin?*
    and *Wasn't that clever? They don't call him Lord
of the Flies for nothing.* So we're dead, we were never really
    alive anyway, and death's okay except for the
putrefaction, the flies, in fact, the maggots of dissolution
    picking the last flecks of beauty off the rickety

quorum of bones, our home base, lovely aggregation of flesh
    and blood. *We want our bodies back,* we scream,
religion's clarion call, but if you ring Heaven,
    use a rotary dial. They're Luddites. The number's
666-SINS, if you were thinking about being good. Think
    again. It's inconvenient,
turning your back on temptation, luscious goddess
    of the lickable mouth. Forget virtue, it might upset your
uneasy tango with present moment, and as your enemies circle,
    remember the Good Book,
vengeance is mine, saith the Lord, an eye for an eye,
    a tooth for a tooth,
which is my point exactly, because no matter what you think
    as you surface for a final breath,
exactly how much do you want to know about yourself? No matter
    how much you think
you know, Satan's still slicking back his hair, shining
    his wingtips, smoothing his
zoot suit, sharpening his square root, because every day
    is party day in Hell.

CRUELTY

April, like any other misbegotten month,
begins with a sprig of hope. Spring, what a laugh,

cordoned off between Antarctica and hell.
Desire's the least of our problems. Pell-mell

egotism's the rotten canker. *Me, me, me,* we lament,
forgetting the finality of our predicament,

gestures of death abounding, murders, stickups,
hysterical rants, so I long for the corrupt

insect hymn of August with its narcoleptic
jaded allure. We met at summer's end, in a septic

knot of already plighted misery, fell in
love so hard, like Cossacks or merciless djinn,

marauding and brutal, panting as spent
nights wrapped around us with reptilian intent.

Or was it less rapturous than I remember?
Perhaps, who knows now or cares? Let us say, our

quiet lives were shattered forever, dismembered,
ruptured before anyone knew what mattered,

suns abandoned, moons embraced, irritable days
together. Was it more difficult to leave than stay,

unforgiven to the end? Who knew that love's sweet
venom could last so long, be so changed in retreat?

We were cruel to everyone but each other in our
exile, and we remain in that desperate bower,

yielding to the indifferent sky, its metallic
zinnia-red clouds like the scribbling of abstemious monks.

Dad, Dave, Deluge, Death

After any visit to Hawai'i, I begin to call my husband Dad,
because his name is David. Dave, Dad, Dad, Dave, and you

can imagine how much a man might like being addressed as
Dad by his affectionate if absentminded wife,

especially a man who has read the works of Sigmund
Freud. Not much to figure out there. So I say, to myself,

Girlfriend, get a grip on yourself, and you say, *What's
Hawai'i got to do with anything? It's where my parents live,*

I reply and remember going to my mother's favorite
Japanese restaurant, the one with the fishpond in

Kaimuki. My brother's there, too, and his son,
like an Easter chick with his closely cropped blond hair,

my mother picking at her food, as usual, and I
notice how much we all look alike, which is kind

of wonderful and hideous at the same time. While we have
pupus and drinks, Tommy and I discuss the sushi menu,

quail eggs, octopus, mahi mahi, sea urchin, a California
roll or two, futomaki, and it's raining torrents,

seismic undulating sheets of water from the sky,
tsunamis of rain, as if the world were ending, umbrellas

useless, and I remember another restaurant, another storm,
vivid as life, a man across the room abandoning this

world, the space between us parting like a curtain, paramedics
extricating his body from the tangle of chairs, his friends

yelling, and the world plodding on, while everyone we love is
zipped into the cool black plastic cocoon of death.

Elliot and I Discuss Eliot via Macbeth

Apeneck Sweeny would hate a boy like you, my chicken,
bookish, beautiful, only ten and thinking about Shakespeare.

Counting the pages of the collected works, "1,527," you say,
delighted, as if more pages meant more pleasure. And as for Mr.

Eliot, out of the blue you ask me about the poet
for whom you are named. "The spelling's different," you say.

God, let's hope that's not all, because as much as I love
his work, Old Possum leaves a lot to be desired as a human being.

In fact, we all do, but you, my monkey boy, having
just discovered Macbeth, memorizing the first scene, witches

keening, "When the hurlyburly's done, when the battle's
lost and won," and when I tell you the story, you cry,

"Macbeth dies?" Well, it's the only way, my darling,
no one could live after what he had done: Duncan murdered,

one by one Macduff's pretty chickens. When we go to see the
play, you revel in the hacking swords, and I think of Four

Quartets: is all time eternally present? It might as well be,
rapacious and inconsequential as the days unfold, dazzling,

squalid, upright and prone. I feel the primordial ape in my bones
today. I want to drag my knuckles on the ground, snort,

until I see your sunflower face watching Macbeth's beheading,
visceral and sublime. And where will all this take us?

"What might have been and what has been point to one end":
exit, stage left, Macbeth's head rolling, and we want to be good,

yet sometimes our passions get the best of us, my sweet, our
zest for the unnatural makes us everything we are not.

Footbinding as a Way of Life

Anxiety, my best friend, a journalist
by trade, clues me in to the latest cataclysms,

cascading waves tall as tenements where
derelicts are set on fire by bands of feral boys,

eros crushed by belief, its celestial
flames quenched in the River Jordan,

godless, god-filled, god-forsaken—
hallelujah, I'm in hell, my meandering

idle mind the devil's workshop, for I'm
Jonah in the belly of God's great

killer whale, a virgin on a moonlit
lycanthropic night, my beloved, the dapper

Mr. Hitler, Idi Amin, Pinochet, repulsive
necrophilic road kill of the century.

Oh, Ophelia, my dear departed sister,
perhaps you can identify my present

quicksand, the queasy suck, the diabolical
rat-a-tat-tat of bullets through my silver

suburban windshield, the not-so-thrilling
tick-tock of time, overlord of the terminally

underwhelmed, trembling stolid multitudes,
vagrant blood wanting to be undomesticated,

wild, but petrified, afraid of the untrammeled
exegesis of evil yammering in our ears,

yellow-bellied to the end, trails of slavering
zombies on the television screen of our dreams.

Gospel

Alleluia, sisters, the time is ripe to send all
boychiks to coliseums, as audience and gladiators, because

camellias are blooming in the corners of our cranial
delirium, milky violet-shot blooms, but a voice from above,

earthy, nasal, says, Let's go dancing, girls, let's
fly into the arms of gigolos, Lotharios, Casanovas, bums,

good-for-nothing musicians. Let's keep wolfhounds, secrets,
harem mentality, painted nails a message to the sultan

indicating the curse is upon us, as it so often is,
jackal mouth open, canines sharp, our beauty stolen by that

kleptomaniac Time, leaving us with the pathetic, hocus-pocus
legerdemain of mascara wands and rouge. We have gotten fat

minding the business of others, while our own mines are
neglected, silver-veined legs given over to varicose,

osprey beaks appearing in the mirror where formerly
plump flesh glowed and lips once resplendent with kisses,

quibbling now over twenty cents with the corner grocer,
redeeming coupons with the passion once brought to

sex. While looking at nudes of Georgia O'Keefe you overhear
two elderly women. "Oh, my Gawd," one squawks and you

understand. The human body is losing its allure,
vacating the premises of erotic compulsion, when every

wish was soaked in the senses. Yet how you miss the sheer
excitement of skin, desire crawling up your spine, the

yammering chaotic chant of your own gaudy Babel,
ziggurat of terror in a Chinese red dress and stiletto heels.

Hatred

Abracadabra, says Mephisto, the firefly
buddha of Rue Morgue, and the whole wide world

changes from a stumbling rick-rack machine
doing the rag time, the bag time, the I'm-on-the

edge-of-a-drag time to a tornado of unmitigated
fury. Yes sir, we are trampling out our vengeance,

grapes-of-wrath time is here again when I think about
Her Majesty, myself, all alone on her throne, tiara askew,

inconsistently worshipped, even by herself, and I could
just die to think how I betray myself in the great

Kabuki theater of my mind, the No Theater, so to speak, but
latitudinal issues aside, here I am starring in a

mystery play. Everyone's in place—cows, shepherds,
no-good-rotten Herod and his ridiculous Roman soldiers.

Only the savior's missing, so what's the point,
putti aside, of the whole big preposterous

Quattrocento mess, the fights, the plague, the frivolous
rococo results, postmodern la-di-da incarnate?

So what's a girl to do when stuck in the last vestiges of the
tawdry twentieth century—have a drink, a fling, say

Uncle? Oh, there's no loathing like self-loathing,
vox populi, vox dei or something like that. I'm rejecting

Western thought here, monotheism included, shuddering as
xenophobic clouds gather over the darkening earth, yeah,

yeah, everyone hates someone, me included, cowering in my
Zen bomb shelter, longing for a thermonuclear whack.

Irony Waltz

Abbott and Costello are dancing cheek to cheek to "Bewitched,
Bothered, and Bewildered" as the new century commences,

confetti drifting down from God knows where, and my desire,
divided in halves, and which I now wear as

earrings, whispers instructions on how to finesse, i.e.
finance my empire, such as it is, rent, phone bills,

groceries, ritual ornaments for protruding body parts:
hands, wrists, neck, earlobes. Bracelets jangling,

I realize I will never be out of debt,
just as I have the concurrent epiphany that I am rich in

kimonos, 47 at last count, and I hear my mother say, "Young
lady, who do you think you are?" To which I reply, "Lady

Murasaki?" This is a big improvement over Friedrich
Nietzsche. Those were the days: chatting about the will to power

over veggie burgers with boyfriends so addlebrained
propinquity is the only explanation for my adoration. Now in my

quasi-Japanese phase, I have a samurai husband, a great warlord,
rigorous and infallible, his calligraphy sublime, down

strokes masterful yet lyrical, as is his secret recipe for
teriyaki chicken, our backyard grill the scene of furious

undercurrents of passion and practicality. A great woman
visits her gloriosity on the world intermittently; a dull

woman lives a life of domestic bliss; and we pirouette to this
exacting choreography, decade to decade, with lords, with fools,

yearning for a poet in a conquistador's armor, or thus spake
Zarathustra, the Übermensch, and he knows where we live.

JANE AUSTEN JAMBALAYA

Anne Elliot—the most perfect woman in *la letteratura inglese*
   after Dorothea Brooke, unless you have a soft spot
   for unscrupulous social climbers like
Becky Sharp and Lizzy Eustace—is in love with Colonel Brandon,
     (Signor Aficionado di Nubile), who, alas, has cast a
   lurid eye on Georgina Darcy, while Henry
Crawford, he of the sinister curling moustaches, lusts after
   our virginal if otherwise impeccable Anne,
   who is also ardently sought by that
dastard Willoughby (what can he be thinking of),
   both Bertrams, bumbleheaded Tom,
   old Sobersides now, and his younger brother
Edmund, quadrilateral cleric and rather sweet
   stuffed shirt, who has slightly more of a chance than
   the others, which leaves our little
Fanny Price rather out in the cold. Oh, well,
   she can become some weird Mrs. Danvers
   in a wretchedly written novel of the
gothic renaissance orchestrated by Catherine Morland,
   who ditches Henry Tilney because as a best-selling
   authoress of rubbish she has oodles of moolah whereas
he has only good humor and ethics to bring to the fray,
   decidedly ho-hum when fame, fortune and their
   gaudy acquaintances come calling. Excuse me while
I herd my Janes into some semblance of order.
   (Where's Gabriel Oak when you need him?)
   Okay, here they are: Jane Bennet,
Jane Fairfax, and the authoress herself, not as many
   as I thought. Who for them? Bennet and Fairfax?
   Too boring for stalwart Mr.
Knightley and he too tedious for Miss Austen. It'll
   take a little conniving to find someone for her,

a slight moving of chairs, reminding me of "Miss
Larolles, the inimitable, Miss Larolles." Wentworth?
  Too stolid, too omphallic. Let's have some fun
  and marry Marianne Dashwood to
Mr. Collins, serves her right for being such a ninny,
  and give Elinor to Darcy, but he's not going
  to be happy or even satisfied,
no jollification in that equation. *Pauvre* Darcy, let him
  eat cake, because he can afford it, and
  I'm saving Lizzy for myself.
Oops, selfish, selfish, selfish, because I want Darcy,
  too. Let's send all my lovely couples
  on an outing to Box Hill, a hideous, transmogrifying
picnic, where the only thing missing is a gale force wind.
  Oh, the squabbling, backbiting, rambunctious
  machinations of the mismatched,
quite a pretty sight to set before the king, or not, given
  the wounds inflicted, both epidermal and psychic.
  No cotillions or balls for a fortnight, so there.
Round up the guilty. Well, *c'è facile,* because if you're
  human you're implicated in bad behavior,
  recriminations, shame, and let's face it,
sisters are the problem here, the Lydias, Kittys,
  Mariannes, Elizabeth Elliots, Mary Musgroves,
  silly, stuck-up, goofy, prone to
tantrums, misalliances, musical talent, morbidity,
  rank-and-file wrong-headedness, wringing of hands,
  reading trash like *The Mysteries of*
Udolpho, and the mothers: grief-stricken, ridiculous,
  poor, oversubscribed to childbearing, dead,
  and the fathers: ironic, hypochondriac, brutal,
vain, not much to work with there, and the villains,
  not really what you'd call evil
  in the sense of Satanic, more ambitious

wastrels, our Willoughbys, Wickhams, Frank Churchills,
    né Weston, Mr. Elliots, a charming,
    gold-digging group, handsome to a fault, super-
excellent bad guys and easy to cast for the movies.
    I see Wickham as an Errol Flynn
    and Willoughby as a dapper
young Clark Gable, tuxedoed with that cool smile.
    Let's give him Mary Crawford, lovely and amoral,
    well dressed, rich, a little
zaftig, unlike flatchested Emma and Lizzy, but attracted to
    sticks, every one, and what's Miss Machiavelli to do
    with them, the anhedonic, Bible-toting bunch of Tory prigs?

Kamehameha Drive-in, 25 Years Later

Aiea, sandwiched between Pearl Harbor and Waipahu, scene
    of my adolescence, soundtrack
by Bob Dylan via Jimi Hendrix, "All along the Watchtower,"
    those initial
chords vibrating still through my bones with the first
    rumblings of
desire, more romance than eros, and an urge to move
    away from Hawai'i, anywhere, somewhere
exotic, like England in the nineteenth century,
    having just seen
Far from the Madding Crowd at the Kam Drive-in, a perfectly cast
    movie, with Alan Bates as
Gabriel Oak, Peter Finch as Farmer Boldwood, and angelic
    Terence Stamp as Sgt. Frank Troy, before
heroin, drink, and chow stole their beauty
    and transcendence, and,
in what was probably her best role, except maybe *McCabe
    and Mrs. Miller,*
Julie Christie as the celestially christened Bathsheba Everdene,
    but I am immersed in a world of mangoes,
kimchi, plate lunches, nori rolls, li hing mui.
    My best friend
Lynn has Hodgkin's disease, and when we meet, shows me her bald
    spot from radiation though she still looks like Ali
MacGraw but without the crooked tooth. Who has crooked teeth
    these days?
No one, as a matter of fact, but me. Lynn and I talk poetry
    and boys,
only I don't realize until later that no one is really talking
    poetry but me, but we're eating
popcorn and discussing metaphysics when Lynn and I go back
    to see Frank Troy walk into the sea,

quivering with grief and cold, and I hardly know what it is
  to be cold, sitting on the hood of my dad's old
Renault with the tropical sky moving like another film
  behind the screen,
seething with emotion so raw that I will run to the library,
  take up Hardy and his crew—
Tess, Jude, Eustacia Vye—and never let them go, forgetting
  how it all began
until 25 years later, looking for sushi take-out with my sister,
  I see the marquee and remember the world of
VW vans and bugs, a world in which Lynn is still alive,
  her flutey laugh echoing over palm fronds as
we gaze down the aisles of sputtering boxes at the cars
  filled with sleeping children, exhausted lovers in their
exodus from the drive-in, but we stay until the end, aimless,
  wild with being young in the
year of grace 1969, that paradisal moment when we would
  see a movie, then go to
Zippy's or swim naked in the Pacific Ocean and imagine
  our endless lives beyond.

Laudanum for Everyone

Arcadia, my Watteau-engorged paradise of earthly delights,
beetles and dirt daubers, dragonflies and hornets,

choreography by Monsieur Balanchine for the Marquis de Sade,
dancers, bleeding but cheerful, feasting on aphid remoulade.

Eight days to the end of the world, eight minutes
from the shores of heaven, eight seconds to eight, finite

gestation of time: slow, slow, fast, fast, over and out. I am
howling with pain, or is it laughter? Both are jammed

in with the bright ideas, flights of fancy, nagging worries,
junkie dementia, mental predicaments of all kinds. I'm so sorry

Kafka had that roach boy wiggling around inside
like a hoochie-coochie dancer on amphetamines riding a

motorcycle up his spinal column. That bug's in me, too,
never sleeping, robust, so what am I going to do in lieu

of opium? I have no fresh thoughts, being fixated on
poppies since we lived in France, huge fields gone

quiet with red, if red can be silent, if red can be
righteous, then I am Saint Joan of Arc, crimson, burning, see

sepulchral greasy remnants of me in the autumn air. I fear
these days like gowns in dreams, too transparent, too sheer

under the blinding light of the midday sun. I'm not feeling
very well today, nor are my best friends—myself and me,

we're lying doggo together like Donne's lovers in "The
Extasie," but with one body and three souls. Me

yodels like a banshee, I'm dignified, and there's craven Myself,
zookeeper at the monkey house, chimpanzees below the belt.

Midnight on the Piazza della Signoria

Ammannati's Neptune stares past the Palazzo Vecchio
    where Bronzino's portrait of *la poetessa* Laura
Battiferri is hidden away in the Quartiere del Mezzanino,
    and after ten years of trying I've just seen it and
Caravaggio's *Decollazione di San Giovanni* with only ten
    or fifteen other people, a miracle in Florence
during the summer, when sunburned hordes roam the streets,
    cameras dangling like goiters,
engines of commerce whirring, buses belching fumes that smother
    the pink and green marble Duomo. Yet all that seems
far away now on this cool piazza, once crowded with
    belligerent towers like San
Gimignano, brought into truculent submission by the Medici,
    as day is conquered by stealthy night
hitherto hidden in the sun's corona, like the gold leaf
    crowns on the Virgin enthroned
in the Uffizi (I'm thinking of the *Annunciation* of Simone
    Martini). The street performers are still out,
jugglers surrounded by straggling groups of irritable
    children, up too late,
kicking soccer balls across the expanse of stone, bouncing
    them against the fence around the
Loggia dei Lanzi. Sitting in a café this is our panorama:
    the copies of Donatello's *Judith and Holofernes*,
Michelangelo's *David,* and the boxed-up bronze of Cosimo di Medici
    that's being restored, and I remember our first
night in Florence, this piazza crammed with people,
    and a chorus (with full
orchestra) was singing Beethoven's *Ode to Joy,* which resonates
    on all the other days as we walk
past the postcard carts, the carriages with their heavy,
    snorting horses, through

quirky bursts of weather. One sweltering afternoon
    in July, I sat in Café
Rivoire and watched the sky fall in dark walls of rain,
    washing the people away like
silt until the piazza was clear, a baptism, a laundering,
    a watercolor. But the sky is clear
tonight, the stars, *le stelle*, cluttering the dark dome
    of the heavens
until the lazy sun remembers its way back into ascendence
    over the craggy tower of the Palazzo
Vecchio, which we pass, stepping on the spot where
    Savanarola was burned,
walking by the shop window glowing with purple and crimson
    gloves, down the Borgo degli Albizi
expecting nothing but dark streets when we turn a corner
    and before us looms Brunelleschi's dome, formidable
yet shimmering like a space ship or the elaborate gâteau
    of whipped cream and liqueur-soaked cake,
zucotto, and I want to break off a piece, devour it and drink
    the whole star-drenched sky beyond.

Noli Me Tangere, Stupid

Are we all clear on the differences between the sexes,
    sociobiologically speaking?
Boys want beauty because they can spill their seed anywhere;
    girls want brains, because their impulses
center on a baby surviving, but this is no help
    when we begin the mating ritual, a/k/a
dating, and the boy is only interested in the one thing,
    while you (the girl) are
enraptured by movies, books, art, theater, clothes, dancing,
    and there you are with a boy, his
focus scrambled by hormones, and you go to dinner
    and he says nothing.
Girls, you know this is true, you get in the car with a
    boy or man and six
hours later you surface as if released by terrorists,
    weary but happy to be alive.
I remember being dropped off in front of my parents' house
    and walking to the door,
jaw aching because I'd been talking nonstop for four hours,
    and then my date would want to
kiss me. Forget it, my face hurt too much, I couldn't pucker
    even if I had wanted to and I didn't.
Lysistrata had the right idea, there's no something for nothing
    in this world or so
Mr. Willis Moore said in his lecture before taking our eighth
    grade drama class to see the play,
not something that would happen today in any classroom
    of fourteen year olds,
or perhaps it does in some corner of the universe where
    conversation is not a lost art,
perhaps in a rarified pocket of Sweden or Nepal,
    nothing like our present

quagmire of blood sports and acquisitive redistribution
    of consumer goods—microwaves, espresso machines,
radios—where speaking to one another is an unpracticed
    art. Take the example of my teenaged
son: dining with him is like eating with Charles
    Bronson in a prison movie,
twenty questions gets you twenty answers and not much else,
    except the sound of a Hoover,
until his plate is clean. This is a boy who once upon a time
    and not so very long ago had a decent
vocabulary, smiled, did not look as though he were auditioning
    to be part of the Aryan Brotherhood.
What happened to him? Will he suddenly turn sparkly
    and vivacious, and
exactly when will this miracle occur? Until the great god of
    utterance rains down his mercy on
young men's heads, I want a war, I want young women to be furious,
    militant, I want them to scream,
Zip up your pants, Romeo, and talk to me, in sentences,
    and I mean right now.

Origami Ragtime

Arigato, sweetheart, so here we are again in the up-tempo
blue-note auditorium of conjugal bickering, sound system

controlled by Mister Moody, dimmer switch by yours truly,
dénouement written two hundred years before by desperate

émigrés from Ireland and Allemagne with accents of inglese,
francese, and hard-drinking pow-wow native Hunkpapa

gitche-gumees, shaken not stirred into a DNA cocktail,
hold the olives, that makes us so very miserable, but

infrequently, thank Jehosaphat, or else we'd take a leap, a
jump on the Japanese bandwagon and fold ourselves hiri-

kiri into a silver bird, flap our wings like Zeus, transmuted,
looking for Leda, Hera hot on his trail, knowing her

man but driven mad by jealousy rather than revenge. No, it's
never that bad, and once rising from the tempestuous

ooze, we're full of vows, no more martinis, no picking up
Pandora on a rainy night, and always follow the Marquess of

Queensberry rules, dukes up, but that's a load of tommy
rot because dirty fighting leads to the boudoir, where all love

sick pugilists go for balm, which the body dishes out
tout de suite while the mind would rather truss itself

up in a Sadean costume, black leather and whips of pious
virtue betrayed, never remembering that love or its

wily surrogate passion has a biological agenda, the equation for
ecstasy written in every cell in the body, so while we're

yelling like kamakazis, I'm thinking, Where's my baby, my
Zeus, it's your Hera, darling, your milkmaid incognito, redux.

Pas de Deux with Incubi

Arrhythmia is the first sign, the pathetic irregular
beat of the heart, pounding like the drums of some lost

cannibal tribe. Amazonian or African, what's the
difference? Eating is eating, unless you're French, then

eating's religion, the table your altar, knives,
forks, spoons ready for the next sacramental flourish,

garnished with dollops so delicious you forget your
heart's basic squeamishness and gorge on the chocolate

iced gâteau of lust until love rises like a viper,
jilts you or, worse, opts for slow torture. Forget eros,

kiss it goodbye, being alone is so pure, the atmosphere
like diamonds, cool, cork-lined as the chamber of your dear

Monsieur Proust, cataloguer extraordinaire of amour's
nocturnal cravings, its need for praise and jealous

oratory, lavish gifts of blood and real estate. You blame
poetry for your predicament, as if a couplet or boxy

quatrain could trip the truly nimble. Perhaps your flat feet
are to blame, the slow pedestrian way your mind

squanders its bright abandon on baboons, narcoleptics,
two-bit philosophers of liberation theology. Freedom,

unkind word, as if anyone could be free from the cryptic
vain musings of other souls. No, you'll meet someone, he'll

walk you home through the spring night, the scent
exactly like a million other fragrant nights on Earth.

You'll be elated, and he might as well be speaking Hindi,
Zulu, one of the hundreds of dialects you'll never understand.

Quel Scandale, Darling

Addressed to a select few, the letter arrives,
but everyone knows about it before noon the next day:

Carrie calls Jasmine in New York, who calls
Delores in Chicago, who tells my brother, who calls me.

"Edith," he says, "Have you heard about
Fatima's letter?" As a matter of fact, I have, but,

gosh, who am I to spoil a fellow's fun, since Fatima dumped
him for the boyfriend she dumped for the letter writer, who

is also history. Mordred, the letter writer, after being
jettisoned by Fatima, has decided to let all her friends

know what she really thinks of them, but they already know, at
least about everyone but themselves, because Fatima

may be indiscreet, but she's not stupid; however, there is the
nymphomania. How dim could her boyfriend be? I'm

out of the loop and even I know about the intellectual surfer,
playwright, Joyce scholar, Marxist, 3 carpenters, the scruffy

Quaker, and, of course, Mordred, the letter writer, who is
resentful with a capital "R." "I knew Mordred when he was gay,"

says Rolly, laughing. "You don't fuck with us." At a
Thanksgiving party Fatima corners me in the bathroom,

unsnaps her bra, says "Who will want me with breasts like these?"
Vincent asks me, "What did they look like?" "Like breasts": I

was more interested in getting her back into that bra than
examining her chest, and anyway she started crying,

"Your brother always made me feel good about my body."
Zut alors, ze body, she make us crazy, n'est-ce pas?

REICHSFÜHRER BLUES

According to Adolf, it was the time for all good men
    to come to the aid of their dictator,
bully boys in charge, certain they were right on the money
    as far as those creepy intellectuals were concerned,
commies, hopheads, an anathema to our paramilitary
    bourgeois blondness,
don't you know, so many things: a thousand and one
    everyday uses for
ether, the orderly distribution of certain elements to the other
    world. *Si, si, si,* it's the
fascist life for me, but, of course, it's not right for
    everyone, take
gypsies, for example, the rules would just get them down—
    no stealing—forget it.
Heave ho, heave ho, it's off to bake you go, and we go
    to our fresh millennium like
Icarus to his new life, a paradise without undesirables
    of all kinds:
Jews, reds, queers, polacks, and we're using modern
    technology to spot them,
klieg lights patrol the outer perimeters of our sociological
    perfection, more
like Utopia than anything Sir Thomas More ever dreamt of,
    less spiritual, a little
more work, but worth it in the end, don't you think,
    and speaking of not thinking, there's
nothing like a uniform to make you feel fine, spic
    and span, sharp,
oleaginous hair slicked back like a black torpedo,
    dangerous, damnable, desperate, yet
piquant, too, like sugar on an arsenic gâteau,
    though you do feel rather

queasy after wolfing the whole thing, this little pig
    went *oui, oui, oui,*
right into the barbed wire quadrangle, what a lovely fire,
    kaboom, bap-bap-bap-bap-bap,
so what if a few Caravaggios are incinerated, so what if
    a few million perish,
the world must be purified of all its flaws, race music,
    jazz, we want wholesome
uncontaminated tunes, soaring melodies as the bombs drop,
    B-52s diving with the big-chested
Valkyries, us *über alles, über* Czechs, frogs,
    wops, Japs, krauts,
Wagner straining in the background, but he's dead, defunct,
    deceased, as we will all be one day
excised from the human predicament and when surveying the
    carnage pundits ask why? It's hard not to stifle a
yawn, because it could be chalked up to illegitimacy,
    punitive war treaties, unemployment, or simply
zeitgeist, I mean, Stalin was just gearing up, and Pol Pot
    a student in Paris. It's the spirit of the age.

So Long, Roy

Apropos of nothing it seems, I burst into tears on reading
    "Roy Rogers Est Mort," or maybe it's
because I'm living in Paris and homesick or more likely
    that Roy looks just like my dad who's had
cancer three times and lives in Hawai'i, and I'm ten thousand
    miles away and the last time he called, my
dad, not Roy, he sounded tired and confused and not
    at all like the tall,
elegant guy I remember from childhood who erased that image
    as soon as he opened his mouth, speaking
fractured French and making goofy jokes, and I think it must
    be the Cherokee blood
giving them both that heap big handsome cowboy look,
    but what made him laugh after going through
hard knocks right and left, the Depression, dead father,
    careless mother?
Is that why they both turned to religion, stopped calling
    on Jack Daniels, switching to
Jesus? Who wouldn't after seeing a world gone mad,
    the camps, a crazy
kamikaze pilot hitting a ship in my dad's convoy,
    and him watching it sink into the South Pacific
looking on as almost everyone aboard died, most of them still boys
    yanked from factories and farms,
men burning to death or drowning because other men
    wanted to rule the world,
not that any of them succeeded, and after the war my dad
    was stationed
on an island in the Philippines, and because he didn't play
    cards began to read
poetry, memorizing great hunks of it, which he recited
    as my bedtime stories,

quoting "The Shooting of Dan MacGrew," and still doing it
    over the telephone, asking how my students like
Robert Service, and I not having the heart to tell him
    I don't teach
Service but a bunch of feel-bad moderns like Eliot and Pound,
    great lover of Mussolini,
two wretched anti-Semites, whom suddenly I see through my dad's
    eyes, which are growing dim,
unfocussed except on the past, where he's still a young man,
    his life an adventure, ups and downs,
victories and defeats, moving from Oklahoma to California,
    singing in bands. Go
west, young man, go west to Alaska, Hollywood, Hawai'i,
    marry decent Christian women, pretty women,
excellent women, buy suburban bungalows, father children,
    entertain them with your stories, your poems,
your shows, but for God's sake don't die and let them see your
    photograph in the newspaper, *le journal, die*
Zeitung, so the whole world can remember your smile and how great
    you looked on a horse.

Trigger Tries to Explain

Aw, Dale, he didn't mean it when he said I was the
best thing that ever happened to him. If he even said it,

chalk it up to the RKO publicity machine. I'm a horse, a
dead one at that, mounted in the museum with glass

eyes and looking a little ratty as the tubby former fans
file by with their bewildered bored kids, who are thinking,

Golden palomino, my ass, I can't believe he brought us
here instead of Disneyland, the boys looking like overgrown

insects and the girls like prostitutes in their halter tops,
jean short-shorts and platform sandals. It would have

killed Roy to see them, being such a goody-goody, always
Leonard Slye just beneath the skin with his Oklahoma homilies,

making everyone feel safe and sound. Oh, sure the big bad
Nazis were gone, but there were plenty of villains left:

on the left the Commies, on the right the McCarthyites.
Poor Dale, you had a horse, too, what was her name? You were

Queen of the West until you gained a hundred pounds on fried
rashers, doughnuts, Wonder bread, and bakery cakes. Okay,

so it couldn't last forever. Get over it, Trigger, I tell myself,
television is fickle. Now it's hospital shows, blood and angst

undercut with tawdry sex. I blame the French, frigging cinema
verité. Where's the story, the hero, the beautiful girl?

Where's the horse? The other dead horses say, Whoa, don't get
excited, Trigger. Nothing's the way it was. That's the truth. Ah,

youth, I try not to be bitter, but sometimes I dream about
Zorro, now there was a guy who could make a horse look good.

UCCELLO, FILIPPO LIPPI, LEONARDO,

Andrea del Castagno, most painters working in Florence were
batty, maybe from indulgence, though Pontormo took it to

considerable extremes, at the end of his life recording his
diet in minute detail, *lunedí: due pesche, pane, e due*

etti di prosciutto, martedí: un melone, well you get the drift,
finicky, misanthropic, but the lord of color, his pink-torsoed,

golden-haired disciple in Santa Felicità, straining to
hold a glowing Christ, giant blue Virgin swooning above,

in the background, a lime-chested St. John, and Pontormo himself,
just to the right of the Virgin, looking squirrely and

kind of lonely, which was probably what he was feeling at
Lorenzo's villa at Poggio, when he collapsed, crying,

"My Bronzino, bring me my Bronzino," and they did or he'd
never have finished his sylvan fresco of Apollo and Diana, an

oculus separating them, as the artist later separated himself by
pulling up a ladder, a prisoner in his own house. When did

quirks explode into a world-rending rage? One day an eccentric
reading something into nothing, the next walking miles of city

streets just to quiet the evil voice inside. How does it come,
the moment when you let go of work, sex, food, a life,

until then things you understand, and they bolt like horses,
visible at a distance but with no connection to the wild

world teeming inside you. Yet how clear your vision is, like
x-rays of paintings in which the position of a hand is changed,

yellow walls converted to mountains, and the father of the Baptist,
Zacharias, becoming an angel of the avenging and implacable Lord.

Valentine for Martin Luther

Arbeit macht frei: well, yes, Germany has
brought so much to the vast cultural

carnival. I'm thinking of you, Martin Luther,
dead 400 years, and not a minute too soon,

either, as far as I'm concerned. Beloved
father of Protestantism: now there's an epitaph.

God, the merrymaking, glorious mayhem, general
hedonism that has been squelched by your two-bit

irascible dime-store vision, women stowed in
jails of domestic servitude, pleasure-loving

kings beheaded and replaced by art-loathing
lugubrious Roundheads with no fashion sense,

moreover, nor any need of it since absolutely
nobody was having an iota of fun. Charles I

once said, "There's nothing more dangerous than a
Presbyterian fresh off his knees." He should have been

quaking in his purple leather, thigh-high boots,
rather than making jokes, right, my dear burgher?

"Squalid middle-class devotion is good enough for us,"
the four-square clerics of Freiburg scream to God, who

understands the value of repression, having used it like a
vise grip since the beginning. Martin, arctic

whoremonger, what can you tell us about sex?
X-rated, of course, but allowed in marriage, though

your wife's breast looks like nothing so much as a
zucchetto, the pope's skull cap, white as Satan's eye.

Woo

Arithmetically speaking, addition is the impulse,
blind electrical charges, chemicals, one cell

calling to the other, but dolled up in the half-lit
demimonde of romantic hallucination, rococo rooms,

eerie music, décolletage screaming, *Market
fresh, dix francs pour deux.* Later you smell the perfume

gone sour, *la nausée,* the cheap champagne
headache, and all your honorable intentions

in the dustbin with the empty bottles, the hollow
jejune promises that mean a lifetime of hell, subsequent

kiss-and-tell of hotel registers, late night
lobbies of indecent longing. If love were a

meritocracy, loneliness would drown the world like
Noah's flood, righteousness a ragtag regatta bobbing

on the waves. Oh, be my turpentine, my slice of luscious
pestilence for which there is no purgative, be the

quim of my greed, delicious vortex of quiet
repulsion at the core of anything beautiful. Be my

soi-disant fire when M. Janvier calls, my recherché
tumble in the hay, my deliberate lie, my rank and file

unworthy attempt at joy, my raspy cigarette
voice on an old LP, the cognoscente of all I despise.

Will you, won't you be my evil twin, my wolfwhistle, my
existential dilemma, though we're two left shoes, my

yin too yang, your yang so turbocharged we have
zero chance of happiness, let's try anyway, whatta ya say?

X-Ray of Your Brain at 4 a.m.

Am I not the most generous of women, so when I turn scientist
    it's not of the mad variety
but for the good of humanity, and I can't sleep anyway because
    of my own rosary of worries coupled with your
cannonade of snoring, so forgive me, darling, if I slip into
    your own most ethereal
dream world, floating on the rhythm of your heart, down the dark
    canal of your most empiric
ear to the moist recesses of Cogito Central, grey palazzo
    of braininess and, well, chaos,
for it's like rush hour on Wall Street after an avalanche
    on the Dow. What's
going on here? The bimbos of memory everywhere, suspiciously
    unclad, as I stick
hatpins in the balloon breasts of all I can reach. This teeming
    foutromanie—
I had no idea this is where you reside each night, a seraglio
    of the senses . . . Not her, that's
Jezebel. Don't you remember your Bible? Ahab may be off chasing
    his whale, but she's still trouble, the
kind that won't go away, except in a dream where, pow, everything
    changes in a second,
like a film edited on acid, Eisenstein gone mad, a jump shot
    to the polio hospital, to Venice, then a flagellant
monk's cell, and you're the holy father, yikes, I never counted
    on this, but it's over soon and on to further
numbskull adventures, taking Khartoum, high-school athletics,
    god, is that boring, rah, rah, rah,
or what about when I show up but like Lolita at the novel's end,
    pregnant, wearing glasses, a Hausfrau,
persnickety, worrying about money, Miss Broken Record, Miss Pay
    the Bills, Miss Bore You to Tears,

quite frankly the most, oh, I'm beautiful again, 26, the age when
   we met, but better dressed,
red velvet mandarin jacket and skin like fresh cream, this is more
   like it, but leaving the ball we are attacked by
salamander people, lizard heads with feet and arms and 18th-century
   Scaramouche costumes, your
tuxedo turning to something Captain Blood-ish as swords clash
   and who knew reptiles could fence
until I hit them on their slimy green heads with convenient
   crockery, and we escape their senseless
vendetta to arrive in an erotic utopia, all peaches and bubbly
   drinks that go right to your head,
which is to say, disable it, and the body has its way,
   ever persuasive, until climbing the
ecstatic peak, we hear a suspicious noise at the door. Uh-oh,
   half naked we scramble out the window, and
yes, it will be nip and tuck as we flee from the slavering
   minions, the razor-fingered armies of
Zocor, evil emperor of Xanax, planet in the system Ranunculus,
   15 million light years from our tranquil life on Earth.

Yellow Fever

Aureole of golden hair, my darling, my shimmering
buttercup, my dandelion, Tweety Bird, dipsomaniacal

canary, too chickenhearted to say chicken shit,
dear bee sting, yellow jacket, sunshine of my life,

elegant, graceful arc of light, Nordic, Swedish,
flaxen, braided, cruel, barbarous, shining inner domes of sunny

gilded cathedrals, gold rush, golden delicious, apple of my eye,
he can do no wrong, no right, no one, nobody

is in a position to revile me as I lie here, inconsolable,
jaundiced, flipping through the yellow pages of my own personal

Kama Sutra of sulfurous yearning, acid, sour,
lemon ice, face like fresh cream, girl with the flaxen hair

meets boy with the sandy crew cut, true love screams
neon sighs—no, signs—sighs come later with the startling

opalescence of birth, bright wail of life turning
picaresque as ego tries on its splendid primrose jacket, no

quelque chose there, and later when rusty with age,
remembering sitting over steaming bowls of gummy

saffron risotto alla Milanese on a honeymoon, harvest moon,
topaz sliver of reflected glory, a slight memory of being

under someone, over someone, someone yourself, where is that
vain creature, that one, who calls Mirror, mirror, on the

wall, plague upon your house, car, yacht, palazzo,
xanthic acropolis of regret called heartbreak, two amber

yolks, rich, heart-clogging ache, muddled gold
zeppelin of heat, distorted luster of my disordered heart.

Zugzwang Amore

Although a chess term, the German word *Zugzwang* or "move
     compulsion" could be used to describe a bad
boyfriend situation, because you have to make a move
     even though it will hurt you,
could hurt him, but probably not since he's a heartless cur
     without morals or at the very least scruples, yet
desirable nonetheless. It's a hip thing, and I don't mean
     in the sense of cool, I'm talking
eros here in its most base and unexplainable form,
     you know, flesh calling to
flesh and all that that entails—ecstasy, tears, hour-long
     telephone calls to a cadre of patient
girlfriends, who say, "Leave the bastard," as if it were
     that easy, because, of course,
he's remorseful, has figured out how to buy flowers,
     and not from the grocery store,
irises, tulips, orchids, daffodils wrapped in great
     swaths of green waxed paper, boxes of your favorite
jellied orange slices, Italian chocolates, an antique silver
     teaspoon. Oh, now he's your perfect
knight, suddenly realizing that John Donne is the way
     to your heart, or Garcia
Lorca, "Green, I want you green," he murmurs in his river
     of *vin rouge,*
Monsieur Mesmer to you, weak and confused, your IQ
     in shambles as you
notice you're considering forgiveness, more from apathy
     than Christian love, although
once or twice a day you find yourself in the middle of a lurid
     revenge fantasy or you
pull out your chessboard and try to remember your once
     glorious game, how you took his

queen in six moves the first and last time you played,
    how furious he was, after
regaling you with his prowess, and you have to admit
    it wasn't a particularly
strategic move, stomping him like an earthworm,
    but on the whole you find the
testosterone thing boring, except in one instance,
    and even that can be exceedingly
underwhelming at times, so when you decide to take him back,
    you find your
voice a little shaky as you form the alien syllables
    which make the
words that lead your most loyal if ironic girlfriend to say,
    "Hold on while I call the
exorcist," but for a time everything is almost normal,
    though waking in the middle of the night,
you think of the strangest things: your beloved, long-dead
    cat Annabelle, or the scene in *Die
Zauberflöte,* the Queen of the Night's revenge aria, sung
    as if her rage-splintered heart will never mend.

III. *Italian Odes*

> O for a beaker full of the warm South
> —JOHN KEATS, "Ode to a Nightingale"

ODE ON MY WASTED YOUTH

Is there anything so ridiculous as being twenty
    and carrying around a copy of *Being and Nothingness*
so boys will think you have a fine mind
    when really your brain is a whirling miasma,
a rat's nest erected by Jehovah, Rousseau, Dante,
    George Eliot, and Bozo the Clown?
I might as well have been in costume and on stage,
    I was so silly, but with no appreciation
of my predicament, like a dim-bulb ingenue
    with a fluffy wig being bamboozled by a cad
whose insincerity oozes from every orifice,
    but she thinks he's spiritual, only I was playing
both roles, hoodwinking myself with ideas
    that couldn't and wouldn't do me much good, buying berets,
dreaming of Paris and utter degradation,
    like Anaïs Nin under Henry Miller or vice versa.
Other people were getting married and buying cars,
    but not me, and I wasn't even looking for Truth,
just some kind of minor grip on the whole enchilada,
    and I could see why so many went for eastern cults,
because of all religions Hinduism is the only one
    that seems to recognize the universal mess
and attack it with a set of ideas even wackier
    than said cosmos, and I think of all
my mistaken notions, like believing "firmament"
    meant "earth" and then finding out it meant "sky,"
which is not firm at all, though come to find out the substance
    under our feet is rather lacking in solidity as well.
Oh, words, my very dear friends,
    whether in single perfection—mordant, mellifluous,
multilingual—or crammed together
    in a gold-foil-wrapped chocolate valentine

like *Middlemarch,* how could I have survived without you,
   the bread, the meat, the absolute confection,
like the oracles at Delphi drinking their mad honey,
   opening my box of darkness with your tiny, insistent light.

ODE TO ITALIAN FRUIT

I am not Charlotte Brontë because I would have died already
in childbirth, the baby dead, too. No, I am in Italy,
    using birth control, a type invented by the Egyptians,
    a scooped out orange half, the hemisphere of rind
a barrier against the sperm, but I digress,
not an unusual occurrence, and I wonder what the Brontës
    have to do with anything, but later I learn I have been
    involved in a brontëesque *collaborazione*
with the facts, creating my own world, with thieves,
turncoats, poetry, danger, and above all good eats

as when in Torre a Mare, a beach town south of Bari,
a roly-poly man on the street warns us as we park our car
    of the black hand, *"la mano nera,"* so we sit
    by the window to watch for blackguards but merely spot
boys strolling with their girlfriends and families,
but no one with scars, tattoos, squinting eyes,
    or coarse malevolent features, and after a glass of wine
    all thought of villainy recedes into a stand of pines
between the restaurant and the beach. After a second
glass we resign all our possessions to the dark world

of disorder, and our talk meanders around maps, routes,
trulli, and a city on the coast of the boot
    heel of Italy, which you think is the site of the famous
    battle of Gallipoli, and I am thrilled to disabuse
you of this mistake, of course, in my best know-it-all
manner, which has so infrequently charmed men in my adult
    life, but I'm on my high horse, off on a tear,
    wondering how something as hideous as war
could be possible in this sublime country,
until you point out that far from peaceful, Italy

has known more butchery than most, that fifty years ago
it was torn by slaughter, led by famous chrome dome
    Benito Mussolini, with whom I share a birthday,
    not hard to believe at times, then, and not precisely
out of the blue, I think of Primo Levi, chemist,
alchemist, and author of *Survival at Auschwitz,*
    which I've just finished reading, a compendium
    of terror that is difficult to imagine
in the midst of so much beauty, yet open any
newspaper and read, for example, about Bosnia,

Rwanda, L.A., and the world seems overpopulated with assorted
monsters. So where am I, in the Italy of skinheads,
    stormtroopers, Neo-Nazis, or the land of Verdi,
    Puccini, Leonardo, and Levi? Both Italys,
both worlds, but I'm saved from my mind by the waiter,
asking whether we want dessert? All summer
    I have ended meals with a wedge of watermelon
    and in a not-so-slightly neurotic fashion have come
to depend on the cool slivers of crimson,
which you'd expect to be called *melone d'acqua* in Italian,

but it's *cocomero,* a silly word but fun to say: *cocomero,
cocomero.* The waiter says he has *lampone, frutti di bosco,*
    and *anguria.* My disappointment is ridiculous. I beat
    down the stiff-armed Mussolini rising inside of me,
order *anguria* because I don't know what it is,
and I can't have what I want, but the waiter brings
    a plate of gorgeous red *cocomero,* so I say, "*Cocomero.*"
    "*No, anguria,*" and suddenly, like Alice, I've fallen into
the Land of Anguria, as in Brueghel's painting
of the Land of Cockaigne, a world in which all things

are given like Moses' manna but infinitely more delicious:
rushing streams of wine, orchards of bread, topiaries

of *gâteau,* and, in my case, a paradise
of fruit: white peaches like globes
of perfume, *pesche gialle,* juicy and orange, grapes,
figs, green and purple, cherries, melons, then plates
of *anguria:* crisp and succulent
at the same time, like love, sex,
food and all things Egyptian and mysterious, which inhabit
their own worlds, some named like the Brontës'

imaginary childhood lands of Gondol and Angria,
and other worlds, anonymous and fiery,
often mistaken for our own
except they are too brutal to be made of the same
ingredients, yet they are, and we are present
as well, smiling, dancing, opening bottles of wine,
eating *ciliegi, fichi, nocilini,*
aranci, mele, kissed by the night,
gazing at the frozen stars as if we will always
drink deep and sleep the sleep of the blessed.

ODE TO MONEY

While looking at the frescoes of the life of St. Peter
    in the Brancacci chapel in Florence,
I hear Megan say the theme of the series is money,
    and I think, you could probably say the same
about most of our lives, having it, getting it,
    spending it, hoarding it, lording it over others,
letting it slip through our fingers, and while most of us
    are not usurers like Felice Brancacci,
who had to commission a chapel to avoid going to hell,
    making ends meet is something that occupies
our minds from time to time, and if time is money,
    is all money eternally present,
or is it the fourth dimension:
    height, width, depth and money?
I'm no Einstein, but I'd say yes, or why are money
    and art thick as thieves,
and while Jesus said render unto Caesar
    that which is Caesar's and to God
that which is God's, sometimes it's not easy
    to figure out which is which, or who is who,
as when Pope Pius made his deal with Hitler,
    or when tax time rolls around, who's god there,
you or the IRS? Because in the Brancacci Chapel,
    when Jesus sends St. Peter out to fetch
a piece of gold from a fish's mouth, I must say
    the fish looks as surprised as anyone,
he's ejecting coins like a slot machine in Reno.
    Most of us have to toil in pretty stony soil
to earn our daily bread, filling out forms,
    counting money, sitting in meetings
so boring our brains turn to liquid
    and drip out our ears, writing gorgeous

sentences for those who would not recognize
    beauty if it announced itself
in full Louis XIV Sun King regalia
    and handed out party favors.
Half the time I'm counting my cash
    like Jacob Marley in hell
and the other half throwing it out the windows
    of Cadillac convertibles while I cruise
through Memphis with Elvis. Oh, simoleons, spondulicks,
    shekels, mazuma, what I wouldn't give for a grand,
a C-note, a sawbuck, two bits, an IOU from anyone,
    even Zelda Fitzgerald, who would probably not
be whispering "Waste not, want not," or "A penny saved
    is a penny earned" into my pearly ear.
In Rome looking at Caravaggio's *The Calling*
    of St. Matthew, there's the money theme again
because Matthew and his repulsive cronies
    are counting coins on a table as Jesus
holds out his hand to beckon the tax collector
    into his doomed if divine fold,
and you've got to wonder what enticement
    he could be offering such a one
as Matthew, because let's face it,
    he would not be saying to anybody, anyway,
any time, you gotta have money, honey,
    if you wanna dance with me.

Ode to Public Bathrooms

After using a bathroom in which it looks as if a murder
has just taken place, I realize the French
    have had one or two terrific ideas
    based on the fact that human beings
are basically squalid and inconsiderate creatures,
or why would they allow their dogs to shit on sidewalks
    I think constantly as I walk though the streets
    not of Paris but of Florence, *not* looking up
at Brunelleschi's dome, the palazzi, handsome men,
shop windows piled high like Ali Baba's cave with shoes,

prosecco, tartufo spread, *pane,* books, antique cabinets,
but *down* at the pavement to dodge the bombs of dog
    excrement that are everywhere waiting
    to attack my chartreuse sandals,
my nun's shoes with a cut-out vamp, *molto erotico,*
because the French know that given half a chance
    we will throw paper, cans, cigarette butts
    on the ground, out the window,
so squads of men in green patrol Paris sweeping the streets,
making it the most beautiful city in the world,

but I'm not there, I'm in Italy, looking down,
contemplating the body, its outward perfection,
    the smooth muscles of Donatello's David
    in a hushed room at the Bargello,
the upraised biceps of Cellini's Perseus
holding Medusa's head aloft in the Piazza della Signoria,
    the marred symmetry of my own feet,
    ten imperfect toes dusted with grime,
trudging along the narrow uneven cobbled street
near Dante's house, dodging a gypsy mother

with her rag-tag band of newspaper-wielding pickpockets,
thinking all the time of the inside of the body coming out,
    like the bronze blood dripping from Medusa's neck,
    necessitating these public rooms,
both filthy and pristine, from the sleek chrome paean
to modernism in Milan to the Turkish toilet
    found in every neighborhood bar with its daunting
    porcelain footprints on either side
of the blackest hole in the universe, dark as the pit
that opens beneath my feet every minute of the day.

ODE TO INSECTS

April arrives on schedule, her foolish sombrero
    studded with thunderclouds,
unfastening her gaudy bolero of green, tender
    with shoots, spikes of iris cluttering the mud,
the new sky hung with giddy fluttering scarves
    of half-starved birds hunting worms
for their squawking young, the orchestral forest
    humming with the trumpet of hawks,
percussion of rain, flutey aria of robins and shrikes,
    harp of wind through the leaves of sycamores and pine.
But the fiddles are missing, buzz of strings.
    Where are my bees, my hornets, my dragonflies,
long-coated Toscaninis in black tie and tails,
    iridescent capes flying behind?
Gone, victims of our lust for lawns, flat expanses
    of rolling green, golf links,
formal mown Gobis gobbling up wildflowers, mallow,
    jack-in-the pulpits, lady's slippers, goldenrod,
fields of yellow black-eyed susans,
    once heavy with pollen and nectar.
Where are my moths, my fireflies, phosphorescent
    cavaliers of summer twilight?
Vanished in clouds of malathion for mosquitoes,
    triumphant as the Ostrogoths sacking Rome,
nocturnal vampire lords, airborne with orders
    from Lucifer for blood.
Where are my monarchs, my moths, my fritillaries?
    Cut down by resplendent fumes,
a once celestial firmament pierced
    by the cry of faster, faster, more, more.
I have let my grass grow, my pavement erode,
    my trees seed themselves in disheveled abandon,

have lazed under giddy dogwoods, lollygagged,
    kissed my darling for no other reason
than that his skin was sweet,
    whispered secret words into the honeyed limbs above:
Byzantium, Belarus, Barbaresco, Botticelli.
    Primavera, queen of this canopy, empress
of all that is new in this old world,
    weave for me a leafy gown
stitched with a hundred thousand greens:
    dusky magnolia, eucalyptus, olive, pea, pitted lime,
the shimmer of a willow hem, a camisole of ferns,
    diadem of fireflies and Queen Anne's lace,
sandals of rough moss, for I am lost in the borders of love,
    the slippery eros of Spring vibrates on my skin,
I dip my finger in the utter nothingness of another's eyes,
    like a perverse mirror, its delirium, its sting.
Oh, honeybee, ecstatic fluff-bodied cross-pollinator
    of almonds and apricots,
my weeds are grown wild
    with spiderwort, dandelions, trillium,
so breed, multiply, lay eggs,
    for everything frilly and perfumed about Spring
is inherent in your minuscule gestation,
    the fruit of your turbulent quivering,
your most tender and malicious art.

ODE TO WARTS

No girl ever sat on her pink and white canopy bed
    and said, When I grow up I want to be a stepmother,
because in fairy tales the operative adjective is wicked,
    and though she's sometimes a queen,
she's the one who makes the girl or someone
    very much like her scrub floors and eat
poison apples or drives her and her little brother
    into the woods and the oven of the wicked witch,
probably a stepmother herself or with stepmother potential.
    And there are the warts.

Most stepmothers have a wart or two (*verruca* in Latin)
    on the ends of their noses mostly
or their chins and one suspects clustered
    on the outside of their hearts.
A doctor told me he often gives children five dollars
    to cure their own warts, and it usually works.
My mother-in-law tells of taking my husband
    when he was a four-year-old to a conjure man
in south Louisiana. She says the old man took her little boy
    into his cabin and talked the warts off his hands.

My own warts were on the bottom of my right foot:
    one of the most difficult things
I have ever done was to walk into an Italian pharmacy
    and say, *"Ho bisogno di una medicina per una verruca
della pianta del piede,"* the woman behind the counter,
    giving me a look as would crush a marchesa,
scuttled behind a curtain to confer with someone,
    and returned with a yellow tube of foul-smelling goop,
though the warts didn't disappear until months later when I read
    they were easily cured by over-the-counter medication.

Doctors! Pharmacists! I was cured by a book.
    When I first married, I read everything I could
about being a stepmother. All the books said I was lucky
    to have two boys because they wouldn't compete
with me for their father's affection. Like most pronouncements,
    I found this to be true and untrue at the same time.
When you are a girl you never think
    you will marry more than once. I remember
my oft-married sister saying before her third wedding,
    "Never the bridesmaid, always the bride."

What is wicked? And what good? A virtuous man can be tedious,
    a spiteful woman lovely,
or any combination you can conceive
    because it's surprising how much you can love
a child who is not your own,
    want so much for his happiness
and yet not want a child at all
    or really anything more than the warts, buboes, moles
that cover you like an ermine cape, your tiara,
    so to speak, the thing that makes you queen.

ODE TO TEETH

My Russian dentist and I discuss poetry,
    well, for a few minutes until he surveys the damage
and packs my mouth with gauze,
    then tells me he prefers Gumilyov to Akhmatova,
how to pronounce Tsvetaeva,
    and don't I agree Mandelstam is sublime,
then he recites something in Russian,
    so I feel pretty darn lucky
that my teeth are a mess because of early decades
    devoted to hard candy and a Grand Guignol
of chocolate bars. Oh, the Paydays of youth,
    the Three Musketeers, Snickers, Mounds,
Almond Joys and a coincidental lack of dedication
    to oral hygiene have left me with an office
of dental professionals as best friends.
    My dentist is apologetic when he causes me
the least bit of pain, but I don't mind
    because, without him and his colleagues,
I would be a toothless hag, or, like Charlotte Brontë,
    a tight-lipped smiler and reluctant
to speak in public, but I am able to sound off
    and voice any number of half-baked opinions
with a set of incisors so pearly
    that I am rarely loath to express happiness,
even laughter, though I'm afraid
    of almost everything—the dark, flying,
driving over bridges, boats, water, heights—
    so you'd think I'd be afraid
of the dentist, but a true show-off
    will put appearance before terror every time.
In the newspaper today I read about a crime
    so repulsive that it hardly seemed human,

yet when I ask my dentist why he left Russia, he says,
    "Oh, life there is insupportable."
Where is it not? I think with something approaching despair,
    though my melancholy can't compare
to Akhmatova's as she battled Stalin's cossacks,
    or Tolstoy's as he waged a holy war
with his own libido: toothless, raping his wife
    just after she'd given birth,
and if a bona fide genius and holy man
    could act that way, how can we expect any more
from run-of-the-mill pedophiles and cannibals?
    Sometimes it's so dark outside
even when the sun's shining. And when are there not monsters
    circling the campfire, howling,
with an appetite for flesh,
    but at least I have my teeth, sharpened canines,
rebarbative incisors, molars of gold,
    so when the werewolves start to close in,
I say, "Come on, Doctor Death,
    let's talk about Pushkin, about Pasternak,
I'm afraid of everything but you."

ODE TO UNTOWARD DREAMS

Have you ever dreamt you had sex with someone
    you aren't remotely interested in,
like a guy you work with or one of your husband's friends,
    and then the next time you see him,
at the xerox machine or a party,
    you're horribly embarrassed
and the poor guy has no idea what's going on
    and neither do you,
because you hardly ever see your husband's friend,
    since his wife can't stand you
because you are childless, thus selfish,
    and your conversation is filled
with utter drivel, like the sex lives of movie stars
    and all your various fears and phobias,
which since she's a psychologist she should find
    at least remotely interesting,
but guess what, she doesn't,
    and she doesn't even know what you and her husband
are doing at night, and the guy at work,
    who could have guessed that he would do
those kinds of things and with such abandon,
    it makes you wonder about his mousey wife
and what's going on there, if anything.
    Freud said all dreams are wish fulfillments,
but sometimes its hard to figure out the exact meaning
    of your desire, though in the case
of your husband's friend,
    maybe you identify with his wife
because in some ways you hate yourself
    as much as she seems to,
though for completely different reasons,
    and the guy at work,

who knows, it was probably the enchiladas picante
    you had for dinner or the four beers,
and maybe you are drinking too much these days,
    though it rarely seems like enough,
your spine crawling up your back,
    like a rat in a Skinner box, shaking so hard
at times you think you either have epilepsy
    or are on the verge of samadhi,
though neither is your dream come true:
    nirvana seems boring
and epilepsy, well, who needs more problems,
    because when we close our eyes each night,
it's review time, *quel calvaire,*
    familiar but hideous,
despite the sexual release with odd partners,
    and running down a tawdry neon street
you find yourself aloft, soaring
    over the paltry world, so far away
it suddenly seems lovely,
    like an intricate toy town,
with tiny perfect people doing tiny perfect things,
    but you always plummet to earth, a hard fall
into the amorous arms of the most peculiar people,
    yet everyone has his attractions,
so when your husband tries to wake you,
    you say, wait, wait, one more fall, one more kiss.

ODE TO BLACK AND WHITE MOVIES

Ida Lupino, my dearest gravel-voiced redhead,
    how many Saturday afternoons have you cracked wise,
fallen hard, picked up the pieces, died like a dog?
    I say "red" but how could I know
except the passionate abandon of your awkward mouth,
    sneering at George Raft,
for your hair, skin, dress, world are grey
    as a February afternoon,
storm howling through the trees,
    while I iron my dad's shirts,
watching Edmund O'Brien, in his pressed suit and tie,
    fedora, cigarette dangling,
driving a big Plymouth through vile neon streets,
    poison coursing through his veins,
feeling D.O.A. myself or like Cocteau's Beauty
    before she found her Beast,
certain I should be wearing dresses cut on the bias,
    dancing with Fred Astaire, trading quips
with George Sanders, learning all about Eve,
    but instead I am spraying starch on collars of shirts
I will never wear, creasing pants,
    pressing sleeves, while watching Fred MacMurray.
Poor schlub, why didn't you see her coming?
    Barbara Stanwyck has betrayal
written all over her beautiful cheap face
    and Veronica Lake glancing sideways
through her blonde waterfall
    at Alan Ladd, fresh from the war,
framed for the murder of his faithless wife.
    Oh, cynicism, incompetence, greed, madness,
mean streets where even the villains
    wear suits and ties. How could I not believe

one morning I'd wake and open a door
    and be someone, anyone other than who I was.

ODE TO BREATH

With a nose like Federico da Montefeltro's
    I'd be capable of real breath, enormous gasps,
elephantine whiffs, rhinoceros snorts, gargantuan inhalations
    instead of the puny gulps, pants, and wheezes
I am stuck with, my lungs like two worn out plastic bags
    from the grocery store, sticky with cherry juice
or nectarine scum, not the muscular pulmonary valises
    of robust others with Herculean bronchia,
Pavarottian larynxes, the inflamed uvulae of screaming infants
    newly alert to the discomfort of life.
Oh, for lungs like Tarzan's to whoop through April
    with its killing beauty, pollen of oak and pine,
sticky marzipan of yellow and gold, to yodel like a Fräulein
    on the Jungfrau, wail, cry, moan like a Greek chorus,
reminding all and sundry of the pettiness of the gods,
    rapacious Zeus, Diana in her bower of blood,
Jehovah in a world-rending rage. What is this catarrh of being,
    this squall in the lungs, the hypnotic rhythm
of in and out, pant of diabolical drums, a continual
    sexual congress between the inside of the body
and the teeming world, radiant with contagion?
    With a neck like Parmagianino's madonna
I could sit enthroned with my enormous divine baby
    in the Uffizi, impervious while hoards gawk,
bombs explode, Titians disintegrate, the pummeled clay
    of Sienna turning to dust again. With a mouth
like Bronzino's Cupid I could ask my mother, Venus,
    for the secrets of love, divine plague,
because I am on the altar of eros again, body weary,
    lungs ragged, lips thin with talk
and the blush of bitterness. With this body
    I can only walk through the world and breathe

its fetid air as if it were some paradise of broken asphalt
and abandoned lots I had come upon unaware.

Ode to Castrati

Who wouldn't want to sing like a diva, a bird,
    a *soprano delizioso,* Violetta, Musetta,
Lucia di Lammermoor—but to undertake amputation for art?
    I speak of the orchiectomy, removal of a boy's testicles
before the vocal cords lengthen and thicken,
    the nomadic adult voice retaining all the animated tone
of a choir boy's but with the saturated brilliance,
    dulcet acrobatics of a woman's aerial *coloratura.*
Yet he's no eunuch guarding the harem. Think of Farinelli,
    Velluti, celebrated castrati pursued by scads of amorous
fainting *signorine,* and the ridge of skin between the anus
    and the emphatic limb crossed by a meticulous horizontal
incision, but that most important appendage still rising
    most importantly so unlike the dark orchid
of the female genitalia, a passion flower
    with its purple labia and riotous tendrils.
As a girl I thought it sad to read the biography of a woman
    and find she didn't have a child.
Now I see that as a child, I thought, what could be better
    than having one of me? How quickly I learned
to loathe my younger self: grubby, ignorant, ungainly.
    Let's consider female castration—inhibiting only pleasure,
not procreation. Who sees the inequity there?
    In a production of *L'Incoronazione di Poppea,*
a mezzo-soprano took the castrato's role. She had breasts
    like watermelons, hands and feet too dainty for a man.
But what is a woman and what a man? Think of standing
    with the groundlings at the Globe, watching *Twelfth Night*
in which Viola poses as a man, but she is a boy
    playing a woman dressed as a man, while being courted
by the lovely if doleful Olivia, played by a boy,
    and the handsome rich Duke Orsino, a man played by a man.

What a stew! What a mole and bat's broth of iniquity
   is this surly ignominious flesh and all its moil.
Who wouldn't give anything for the voice of an angel
   and wings to fly above the rough dirt of birth?

ODE ON MY BITTERNESS

> Because it is bitter
> and because it is my heart.
> —STEPHEN CRANE

"Do you like it this bitter?" my mother asks
    as we drink our first cup of coffee in Paris,
and I have to say, "Yes"—I like the way
    it excoriates my tongue, drives sleep deep into my body
like Rommel into Egypt, marries so sublimely
    with bread and butter, sharpens my tongue
like the poniard of some remorseless condottiere,
    the gold ducats of Cesare Borgia jingling in his purse.
I hold my ire close to me, like an ungrateful child,
    glory in its imprecations,
dearer than affection and caresses, weep for it
    the way Catullus pined for Lesbia,
his hate more gorgeous than his adoration,
    his curses like rubies in a field of stones.
Bitterness clears the mind in a way that happiness can't,
    because you want pleasure to stay a while,
his flesh like new bread, easy to sink your teeth into,
    whereas spite comes as an unwelcome guest,
decides he loves your house, and why not,
    the refrigerator's full,
your conversation sparkles like a polished saber.
    Hatred brings out the best in you,
as it did in Michelangelo Merisi, who, after murdering
    Rannuccio Tommasoni over a tennis game,
fled Rome for Malta, where he painted
    his divine *Decollazione di San Giovanni,*
and in the blood spurting from the Baptist's neck,
    signed his name—"Caravaggio."

How can we hope for goodness in such a world,
    the beautiful acid of sunrise searing our eyes?
To be angry is to be alive, your heart filled
    like a foaming cup with all the wrongs,
slights, innuendoes, backbiting,
    raising it to your lips
like some half-mad member of the minor nobility
    resentful about his place in court,
his philandering wife, his wastrel son, debts,
    meager harvests, plague coursing
through the land like a savage invading army,
    the king is dead, long live the king.

Ode to the Lost Luggage Warehouse at the Rome Airport

Until you've visited the lost luggage warehouse
    at the Rome airport in August, you have not lived,
the Mediterranean sun insinuating itself
    into the inner sucking marrow of your bones,
roasting your epidermis like a holiday bird's,
    a goose, upon reflection, would be the fitting
analogy. You hear the faint sizzling of the fat
    under your skin, organs grilling, brain singed
as you walk to the guardhouse and show the uniformed
    sentinel your paper that certifies you have indeed
lost your bag. You gaze at his amazing hat with plumes
    tinted maroon and gold while he scrutinizes your clutch

of ragged forms, signed by Signor Nardo Ferrari,
    minor functionary with the state airline
at the *ufficio* in Firenze, who has confided
    in beautiful English he will retire at the end
of the month and devote himself to the cultivation
    of vegetables and fruit, a noble endeavor,
but you suspect he'll not be leaving his lush *paradiso*
    to iron out your petty problems. You have come in pursuit
of your bag, supplicant on a holy quest to retrieve
    that which is your own, or was once your own,
the dresses, coat, boots, and intimate et cetera,
    nothing priceless, no treasures as such, but dear to you,

especially the black coat you bought in Paris
    in a decrepit building below Sacré-Coeur,
going with Marie after lunch, giving the secret password,
    hearing the answering hiss, walking up four flights
of stairs to a room filled with ugly clothes,
    one divine coat, now lost in the dark regions
of this Italian underworld, you hope, for if not here,

it's apparently nowhere. This warehouse is a warren
of high-ceilinged rooms with thousands of bags stacked
    on metal shelves, precariously piled backpacks
with scurf from Katmandu, Malmö, Khartoum, Köln, Kraków,
    Istanbul, Reims in France or Francia in *italiano,*

chic makeup cases, black bags like the suitcases of doom,
    hard-shelled portmanteaus like turtles (soft parts
incognito, mating in tandem), briefcases, carpet bags,
    19th-century trunks with straps and buckles,
and you see a woman, *molto dolorosa,* in latex gloves,
    a surgeon delving, methodically, in a suitcase
filled with Japanese snacks—arare, dried squid, rice candy
    wrapped in thin edible paper, red and green jellied
sweets—recognized from your childhood in Hawai'i, and amid
    the *conglomerazione* of heat, memory, and rage you imagine
a Japanese man, thinking, I'm going to Italy, but the food,
    I'll.hate it. Then packing all his favorites: the sublime

shredded mango of blessed memory, cracked plum, dried peas,
    and you think of Sei Shonagun, supercilious court lady
in 10th century Japan, because you are reading her Pillow Book,
    a record of things that disgust or please her,
and you whip your kimono around and say,
    "Things I adore about Rome: the lingerie stores
for nuns with their fifties bulletproof brassieres
    and other medieval undies, the floor of St. Peter's
with its measurements of the lesser cathedrals
    of the world (Milan, Florence, St. Paul's in London),
Caravaggio's *St. Paul* and *Virgin of Loreto.*
    Things that disgust me in August: backpacks with cheese,

child carriers imbedded with the scum of mashed
    bananas and cereal, petroleum-laced breezes
from jet exhaust, the color navy blue." Your Italian

is meager but the denizens of this particular realm
of hell are courteous if lethargic and show you
     that the bags are stacked by month:
agosto, luglio, giugno, but that's as far
     as they go. No Joe DiMaggio or before. To be
anywhere else is all you want. You hate your clothes,
     no coat's worth the flames licking your feet.
You take a careful waltz through the months,
     and find nothing in the midst of so much.

The whole long way back to Florence, while the gorgeous
     panorama of the countryside flies by,
you have a *caffè,* try to read, but a few seats down
     a child screams, hysterical with fatigue,
and you see his face with its sticky impasto of snot,
     candy and tears, and you think of all your losses,
those past and the ones to come, your own death,
     il tuo morto, which makes the loss of a French coat,
shoes, and a few dresses seem ridiculous.
     You think of your arrival in Florence, the walk home
from the station past the Duomo, your husband's hands,
     kisses and the dinner you'll eat, prosciutto

and melone, perhaps some ravioli in a restaurant
     near the Sant'Ambrogio market, you'll buy a new coat
for winter, an Italian coat, *il soprabito,*
     one more beautiful than the one lost. That's the way
your life will go, one day after another,
     until you begin your kamikaze run toward death.
It makes you sick to think of it until you begin
     to get used to the idea. I'd better get busy,
you think, enjoy life, be good to others,
     drink more wine, fill a suitcase with arare,
dried squid. When you leave home anything can happen.
     You may be caught in a foreign country one day,

without money, clothes or anything good to eat,
    and you'll have to try those stinky chitterlings,
brine-soaked pig knuckles, poached brains quivering
    on a wooden platter, tripe, baked ear wax,
fried grasshoppers, ant cakes, dirt soufflés,
    and though it seems impossible, they could prove
delicious or at the very least nourishing.
    Don't make a fool of yourself, and one day
you may join Signor Ferrari in his bosky Eden.
    Everyone will be there God, Jesus and Mary,
your mother and father, even your pain-in-the-ass sister
    who got everything. Heaven, you hate it:

the conversation's boring, and everyone's so sane,
    so well adjusted. And it's cold. Heaven should be warm,
a bit like Tahiti, so you're upset, and then you see
    your sister, and she's not cold because she's wearing
your French coat. But you're not in heaven, you're on a train,
    going faster, it seems, as you approach Florence.
You're in a muddle, glum, have nothing to show
    for your day but a headache and a blister
on your heel. You want the train to crash,
    blow you to kingdom come. You want your mother
to kiss you, call you Baby, Darling; you'd sell
    your soul for some shredded mango or dried plum.

About the Author

BARBARA HAMBY's first published collection, *Delirium,* won the 1994 Vassar Miller prize, the 1996 Kate Tufts Discovery Award and the Poetry Society of America's Norma Farber First Book Award. She is also the recipient of a fellowship from the National Endowment for the Arts and three fellowships from the Florida Arts Council. Her poetry has appeared in *The Paris Review, The Iowa Review, The Kenyon Review, Parnassus,* and *The Southern Review.* She lives in Tallahassee, Florida.